COUNTRY LIVING

750
Style
& Design
Ideas

COUNTRY LIVING

750 Style & Design Ideas

for Home & Garden

From the Editors of
Country Living Magazine

Hearst Books | A Division of Sterling Publishing Co., Inc.

Library of Congress Cataloging-in-Publication Data:
Country living : 750 style & design ideas for home & garden / from the editors of
Country living.
p. cm.
Includes index.
ISBN 1-58816-270-2
1. Interior decoration--United States–History–20th century. 2.Decoration and ornament, Rustic–United States–History–20th century. 3. Garden ornaments and furniture–United States–History–20thcentury. I. Title: 750 style & design ideas for home
& garden. II.Title: Seven hundred fifty style and design for home and garden. III.
Country living (New York, N.Y.)
NK2004.C68 2003
747–dc21

2003006321

Published by Hearst Books
A Division of Sterling Publishing Co., Inc.
387 Park Avenue South, New York, N.Y. 10016
Distributed in Canada by Sterling Publishing
℅ Canadian Manda Group, One Atlantic Avenue, Suite 105
Toronto, Ontario, Canada M6K 3E7
Distributed in Australia by Capricorn Link (Australia) Pty. Ltd.
P.O. Box 704, Windsor, NSW 2756 Australia

Printed in China
All rights reserved

ISBN 1-58816-270-2

For Country Living
Editor-in-Chief: Nancy Mernit Soriano
Design Director: Susan M. Netzel
Executive Editor: Lawrence A. Bilotti

www.countryliving.com

Designed by Liz Trovato
Edited by Pamela Horn

10 9 8 7 6 5 4 3 2

Table of Contents

Introduction

As editor of *Country Living* Magazine, I am continually asked to define country style and suggest ways to get the look. As a decorating style, 'country' has clearly evolved over the years, taking on a broader variety of looks—from rustic to modern—and finding itself equally at home in the city and suburbs. Despite these changes, the essence of country has remained strong and true. It continues to draw on our sense of tradition, recognizing the value of handmade and timeworn furnishings and objects, and finding new purpose in salvaged and discarded goods. It mixes old and new in a casual, relaxed way and often with a sense of whimsy or surprise. Above all, it is a style where comfort is key and self-expression is not only acceptable, but highly encouraged.

In *Country Living 750 Style & Design Ideas for Home & Garden*, we examine the essence of country style today through decorating, collecting, gardens, crafts, and food. From page to page you will see how others have brought country into their lives and learn by their example with inspiring photos and helpful style tips and suggestions. Find out how to choose the right color for you and how to successfully introduce pattern and texture into a room. Learn to mix flea market finds with new furnishings or how to organize your possessions with creative storage solutions. Then discover inexpensive ways to add a personalized country touch to any room.

If you're a collector—and who among us isn't—there are helpful suggestions on how to display and care for your collections. We've also included detailed information on

Country Icons —the objects that over the years have become synonymous with country style. Whether you collect yellowware, teddy bears or Windsor chairs, the information will offer insights into the historical significance of each object and helpful clues on what to look for when shopping for your next addition.

In the garden, there's plenty of inspiration and advice on lawn care and landscaping, decks and patios, and choosing the right fence for your home's architectural style. We've included potting tips, things to consider about climbing vines, and how to improve the bounty of your flower and vegetable gardens with less maintenance. There's advice on borders — green and gravel— and a look at some decorative containers and options for city gardeners.

Since country style is often reflected in handmade products and crafts, we've included some simple projects for you to enjoy. There are easy-to-follow instructions for creating your own personal journal or making a fabric-covered keepsake box for a child, parent, or friend. Personalize your stationery and note cards with store-bought rubber stamps, learn how to make a seasonal berry wreath; or preserve the essence of floral scents year-round with your own special formula of potpourri.

As no book on country style would be complete without food, we've devoted an entire section to the comfort that home cooked meals (some prepared in under an hour) add to our reminiscences and aspirations of Country Living today.

—Nancy Soriano, Editor-in-Chief
Country Living Magazine

Country
Decorating

Decorating Is About Making Yourself at Home

Mixing furniture styles can be tricky, but a few basic decorating guidelines help make it work.

First, figure out a room's function, and then create focal points using art and antiques, accessories, and pattern.

Keep the backdrop simple.

Choose a classic color palette.

Bring in textures that feel good and don't require high maintenance.

Texture comes from materials such as linen, cotton, jute, and "aged" leather that make upholstered furniture comfortable, approachable, and enduring.

Carefully specified details—nailhead trim, button-tufting, leather welting—enhance the mood or offer a surprise.

With large-scale pieces kept solid, classic country patterns show up boldly.

Accessories reflect personal style. The new tripod lamp, cube ottomans, and fire screen pair easily with antiques.

The colors to live with are the colors you love. Use soothing earth tones that will play up bits of color interspersed throughout.

DUCK DECOYS

Once relegated to hunters' sheds, utilitarian waterfowl carvings raised the art of deception to new heights. In January 2001, a hand-carved Canadian goose sold for $684,500 at Sotheby's New York. It set an auction record for a wooden decoy and won the seller significantly more than Cape Cod native, Elmer Crowell, likely earned when he carved the utilitarian piece 80 years earlier.

The craft of creating waterfowl decoys emerged in North America centuries before European settlers arrived on our shores. Native Americans molded reeds, feathers, and other natural materials into realistic forms to lure live birds within hunting range. By the mid-1800s, a cottage industry of crafting carved and painted wooden decoys thrived along the continent's main migratory flyways. Large-scale production continued until the 1920s, when commercial bird hunting—which had driven several species to full or near extinction—was outlawed and sport shooting fell under strict regulation. Although demand among hunters waned, folk art collectors and skillful carvers have kept the tradition alive.

Antiques prices range from a few hundred to many thousands of dollars depending on age, artistry, and maker.

HOOKED RUGS

One of the more cheerful solutions to 19th-century Americans' daily needs was the hooked rug. To alleviate the chill of cold floors at little or no expense, thrifty homemakers combined scraps of yarn and worn clothing with homespun backing to create splashes of color and beauty in dark rural homes. Over the years, the utilitarian practice evolved into a time-honored craft, showcasing an individual's creativity, relating family histories, and encompassing a wide range of styles.

Scholars believe that settlers in the ports along eastern Canada and northern New England were the first to make

hooked rugs. The inhabitants of these harbor towns became familiar with the mats sailors knotted with small, hooklike tools and began experimenting in their own homes with fabric remnants, homespun yardage, and hooks of wood and bone. Because patterns for simple blocks and circles could be created by tracing the perimeter of books, plates, and other household items, many novice craftspeople favored geometric patterns. More ambitious undertakings produced floral designs, portraits of pets and people, and milestones in a maker's life, such as a marriage or birth of a child.

When jute burlap began to be imported from India in the 1850s, North American craftspeople found the stronger backing easier to work with. Not long thereafter, stenciled designs made available by peddlers and ladies' magazines catapulted rug hooking into a national pastime. Late in the 19th century, cottage industries sprang up as rug hookers who had made enough rugs for their homes realized the economic potential of crafting pieces for sale. The best known was the Grenfell Mission, in Newfoundland, established in 1890 by Englishman Dr. Wilfred Grenfell.

The advent of affordable, mass-produced carpets and linoleum early in the 20th century, along with changing tastes, caused a decline in the popularity of hooked rugs. During the Depression, however, thrifty homemakers revived the craft. Ever since, craftspeople have kept the skill alive, both reinterpreting traditional designs and creating their own patterns, reflecting the hooked rug's long, colorful journey from floor to wall.

Prices for antique hooked rugs range from $250 (for a simple pattern dating from the 1930s) to $1,000 or more (for a 19th-century example with an intricate pattern and bold colors).

ADIRONDACK CHAIRS

The broad arms and slanted back of the classic Adirondack chair embody summer's leisurely pace. Generations of Americans have succumbed to its charms, sitting back to enjoy breathtaking mountain views, sunny days at the shore or a break in the backyard. Though its name pays homage to the Adirondack region of New York State, the chair is just as likely to furnish a California garden or the veranda of a Texas ranch. Its appeal lies in its simple slatted design—the back provides just the right angle for dozing, and the broad paddle arms easily accommodate a good book or a glass of lemonade. Take a seat and let summer unfold.

New York's Adirondack Mountain region became a fashionable travel destination following the Civil War. The simple wooden Adirondack chair reflects the region's rustic charm; some experts believe the form might be an adaptation of the Westport chair—a similar lawn chair created by an Adirondack vacationer around 1900. The design was soon patented by a carpenter in Westport, New York, on Lake Champlain, the region's eastern gateway, and the chair began to appear in resort and camp photos. At least 50 red and dark-green chairs once filled the expansive lawn of the posh Lake Placid Club.

Today, Adirondack chairs are widely produced by furniture manufacturers and by amateur and professional woodworkers. Old Adirondack chairs are becoming harder to find, but they often surface at outdoor antique markets during summer months.

Prices range from $75 to $125 and more for examples in pristine condition.

Pieces can be found at the Adirondack Antiques Show, held each fall at the Adirondack Museum, in Blue Mountain Lake, New York.

Tips for a Country Kitchen

Ceramic tiles have been a favorite for floor and wall coverings in country kitchens.

Terracotta flooring tiles are easy to maintain and make for a good transition from wood flooring used in other parts of a house.

Warm your ceramic floor tiles in the winter with a few rag rugs.

Hand-painted tiles used for backsplashes add bright color to a room and stand up well when exposed to cooking steam.

Louvered shutters add a true country feel as they let in both sunlight and garden views.

Let your collections show by using cabinets with glass doors.

If there is room, put a comfy wing chair in the kitchen for good cookbook reading!

YELLOWWARE BOWLS

When yellowware shipments came to America from England early in the 19th century, people eagerly made room in their cupboards. More durable than redware and less cumbersome than stoneware, the newfangled goods were handsome and inexpensive to buy. A staple in American kitchens from about

1840 to 1940, they combined simple good looks with rugged utility. Made of buff-colored clay fired at high temperatures and sealed with a clear glaze, the sturdy pieces have been called the original oven-to-table ware. Early pieces are plain; later pieces are slipbanded—sometimes with sponged designs—or embossed. The easy-to-handle mixing bowls became the lasting favorite.

Today's collectors value these pieces for the warm color they bring to a room. The most valuable are the graduated sets. Although bowls are commonly seen in a nest of five, many are actually produced in eight to 12 different sizes, ranging from about four inches in diameter up to 17 inches

or more. The most valuable pieces generally fall at either end of the spectrum.

Dating a piece of yellowware becomes easier if you brush up on a few key characteristics. The first bowls were thrown by hand on a potter's wheel, but the majority of yellowware from the late 19th and early 20th centuries was produced by using molds. These molds fostered a variety of impressed and embossed designs with floral, geometric, and scenic motifs. Another hint for dating is the lip on the bowl: Nineteenth-century pieces were often fashioned with rolled lips, while 20th-century bowls tend to have a less-rounded lip or a wide collared rim.

Period yellowware bowls with slip bands or embossed decoration range from about $25 to $200 apiece.

Aged surfaces and natural materials take the "too new" edge off renovated kitchens.

Hang blue-and-white transferware or pretty china plates in a row above your windows. (See page 29.)

Cool Colors

Use color to create a sense of continuity in an eclectic room.

Have fun with accessories: Mix functional pieces such as jadeite plates and mugs with purely decorative elements like terracotta flowerpots filled with clumps of wheat grass.

Hang an unframed painting found in a flea market to inspire a color scheme.

Use big white china bowls and wire swim-locker baskets from the 1940s as practical catchalls for kitchen sundries ranging from produce to laundered place mats.

Serendipity in Color

❊ Painting walls and trim in saturated shades of ocher and spruce adds excitement to a 200-year-old room.

❊ Surround yourself with colors that are soothing to you and use them as tools of self-expression.

❊ Try curtainless windows—they show off the colorful woodwork and the outside garden.

Trendy colors can instantly date your furniture and your home. Old blues, greens, and turquoises remain popular from year to year.

Find inspiration everywhere. As you decorate your home, take notice of colors that excite you in nature or in your favorite collections.

BLUE AND WHITE SPONGEWARE

Blue-and-white spongeware won the hearts of American homemakers in the mid-19th century, but the sponge-decorated pottery's most popular color palette was by then no newcomer to Western shores. Blue-decorated Chinese porcelain had been imported since the 18th century; because the wares were costly, English and American potters began to imitate Chinese exports. One of the more rustic forms of the classic color combination eventually was created with pigment-saturated sponges that left charmingly mottled impressions. Spongeware has been produced in a variety of colors over the years, but collectors remain true to all hues of blue—people love it for its fresh good looks in kitchens both traditional and modern.

Rural American households have always needed durable kitchen tableware. Spongeware, widely produced in England and in the United States in the 19th century, could withstand the daily grind subjected to it by large families and community gatherings. By the 20th century, homemakers were stocking their cupboards with affordable and sturdy pie plates, platters, pitchers, mugs, and dishes that could travel from prep site to oven to table. And spongeware's utilitarian forms—mixing bowls, butter crocks, soap dishes, even spittoons—proved as straightforward as its colors—green, brown, and, of course, classic cobalt blue.

Spongeware refers to the technique used to decorate a stoneware or earthenware body: A sponge is dipped in pigment, then applied to the clay surface to create a pattern (stylized motifs are applied with a cutout, shaped sponge). A mottled, handwrought appearance results.

Prices for 19th-century pieces begin at around $150 and reach $500 or more for rare pitchers and other desirable forms. Value is determined by condition, age, color, rarity of form, and the graphic appeal of the sponged decoration.

Use color to create unity and to link diverse patterns
and forms.

Paint the floor an unexpected color.

Painting an assortment of mix-and-match side chairs a favorite color makes them look as if they have always belonged together.

Mix old and new—old surfaces provide texture and permanence. New things add great spark.

Children really respond to color—use it liberally in their domain. Let them pick the colors that make them happy.

The modern paintings juxtaposed with relaxed, vintage-looking furniture create a timeless room.

Practical tables, armoires, desks, side chairs, and beds promise to last forever if you'll just give them a fresh coat of paint or a fun new slipcover every once in a while.

SIGNS OF THE TIMES

There's something heartwarming about a hand-lettered sign that advertises farm stand peaches, fresh eggs, or a small-town ice cream parlor's flavors of the day. Whether it's for their pure nostalgic quality or the old-fashioned, simple messages, these colorful pieces of Americana have long been magnets both for collectors and for the artisans who strive to replicate them.

Advertising is as American as apple pie, and older than the nation itself. Colonial trade signs relied more on symbols than on words to relay their messages. As the nation flourished and literacy spread, simple hand-lettered signs began to advertise the staples of everyday life.

The finest placards were the work of professional sign painters who found steady work as America became increasingly mobile throughout the 19th and early 20th centuries. Decades later, when the Gold Rush lured people out West, new saloons and other enterprises created an explosion in signmaking. Decades later, automobile travel gave rise to roadside ads, and technical developments such as the ability to lithograph pictures and messages on tin allowed signs to be mass-produced.

Many signs were designed for hanging out-of-doors, where they took a real beating from the elements. Even indoor signs were scratched and discolored over time. Today, it is this aged appearance that the collectors look for, and reproductions are fashioned with this characteristic time-worn look.

Hand-lettered signs from the 19th and early 20th centuries range from about $200 to several thousand dollars, depending on graphics and condition. Mid-20th-century signs can be found for less than $100.

Invest Your Whimsy in Seas of Color

A white cabinet holds a collection of 1930s and '40s pottery as well as compatible pieces found during the past 10 years.

A collection of enamelware atop an antique blue buffet can fill a room with charm and summery warmth all year-round.

Use vintage blue-and-white ceramics, textiles, kitchenware and flowers—they reflect the outside surf and sky—and provide undeniable charm.

Seashells help to set off a color scheme of snow white and cream via their natural pinks and corals.

A flea market-find nautical screen adds ambiance to the eclectic collections in this dining room.

Mixed and matched patterns on the walls, curtains and cushions echo the same blue hues found in the graceful caned and bamboo furnishings.

Open shelving in the kitchen provides a great showcase and easy access to lidded containers.

Robin's-egg blue spice jars are lined up to serve as a ripening area for luscious yellow tomatoes.

Making a Lofty Space Feel Like Home

Sumptuous furnishings and natural materials can turn the open spaces of a refurbished barn into a comfortable country home.

A rustic basket for holding firewood and a stained end table flank a modern overstuffed leather divan. The organic pieces soften the finished sofa and make the room feel cozy.

A distressed wooden frame hanging on a barn beam highlights the interplay of natural materials.

Arrange an interesting assortment of small boxes and small wooden bowls filled with spruce cones and dried lavender on a tabletop.

The countryside is echoed in the interiors
with unfinished beams, unpainted plaster walls, and
random-width flooring with a natural oil finish.

In the kitchen, a handmade steel shelf with a hook
holds dishcloths.

Try hanging bookplates of botanical prints in handmade
steel frames to add a touch of the floral to a spare wall.

Use natural materials to dress the dining room table, from slate place mats to textured linens.

A cup, cake stand, bowl, and candlestick all in alabaster form an eye-catching collection.

Large unadorned windows frame views of the wooded countryside.

The array of textures and earthy colors make the bedroom feel rustic and elegant at the same time.

Early 20th-century French iron garden chairs set around an austere wooden table lend an air of playfulness to the dining area.

Rest & Refresh

Fill your bedrooms with your favorite colors and patterns.

You can give your bedroom a quick country makeover simply by changing the sheets.

Dress the box spring in a contrasting sheet that will catch the eye when the sheet is turned down.

To change the mood of a guest bedroom, just change the pillowcases and duvet cover.

Mix and match madras plaids and floral prints with gingham checks and calico cottons.

Little details come together to really personalize the bedroom, such as an antique headboard and fresh flowers on a nightstand.

Ribbons and lace add a touch of elegance and romance to simple white linens.

Give guests plenty of pillows so they can prop themselves up to read or breakfast in bed.

Keep the room simply furnished and in neutral tones. That way, fresh looks can emerge through changing fabrics and patterns.

PAINTED BENCHES

Few pieces of country furniture are as practical as the wooden bench. Requiring for its construction only a few wooden boards, basic carpentry tools, and whatever spare paint may be stored in the shed, this staple of rural American life has been called into use for countless home-and-garden chores for centuries.

These benches served as surfaces for lining up homemade soaps or for cooling canning jars for preserves. Although our daily tasks have changed significantly, wooden benches remain a versatile household accessory.

Homemakers can stack them in decorative pyramids, use them as coffee tables or informal seating, and place them outdoors for potting plants.

Place indulgent comforts into unexpected places. Turn a children's tree house into an adult retreat by tucking away a well-dressed pillow.

Change your cushion covers with the seasons.

Transform a flour sack into a pillowcase.

Turn a pullout guest sofa into a bed of roses— just the place for an afternoon cup of tea.

PLAYFUL COLLECTING

▨ There are no hard and fast rules about what makes a collection.

▨ Mixing and matching colors, shapes, and patterns lends a light and happy air to any room if you cluster pieces and display them with style.

Trust Your Instincts

▦ Trigger the senses by using colors, scents, and sounds.

▦ Painted pieces, bright colors, and layers of patterns should all come from deep within you.

▦ Layers of colorful patterns soak up light.

Herbs perfume the garden, and the aroma of whatever is cooking in the kitchen can be quite intoxicating.

Favorite music piped through your rooms and garden provides a very personal touch.

Create public and private spaces. A living room is a magical place to gather, but bedrooms offer quiet places to read, contemplate and curl up.

COMB-BACK WINDSOR CHAIRS

These were brought to Philadelphia by way of England in the 1730s. The basic stick-and-socket design—in which legs, arms, and back spindles are anchored by a solid plank seat—was copied and then reinvented by Colonial furniture makers, who marketed the modestly priced chairs for use both indoors and out.

By 1760, demand for comb-back armchairs (so-named for the form of the back, which resembles a lady's hair comb) was booming. The "revolution" had begun. Craftspeople in furniture-making centers outside Philadelphia (including New York City, Newport, and Boston) were quick to pick up the torch, reinterpreting the comb-back style well into the 19th century. More than 250 years after its introduction, the American comb-back remains valued for its graceful form, sturdy construction, surprising comfort, and remarkable versatility. Recent interpretations on this classic wooden chair keep it a familiar sight in kitchens, parlors, dining rooms, dens, and offices across the country.

MILK GLASS MEMORIES

I n the late 19th century, many a lady's vanity table held pin trays, cologne bottles, and jewelry boxes molded from opaque white glass. In the 1950s, dining tables were often set with matching dinner plates, salad bowls and tumblers made from the same material. As we enter a new century, this clean white glassware is enjoying yet another wave of popularity.

First produced in this country early in the 1800s, milk glass was presented as an affordable alternative to European porcelain. To make opaque white glass, manufacturers added ingredients such as tin oxide or fluorides to their standard recipes. Originally called opal, the glassware became popularly known as "milky-white glass" or simply "milk glass" around 1900.

Milk glass enjoyed a surge in popularity during the Victorian age, when mechanical glass presses churned out inexpensive pieces in an endless variety of patterns. Late 19th century factories rarely produced complete dinner services, but they did create matching four-piece sets consisting of a

covered sugar bowl, a creamer, a covered butter dish, and a spoon holder, or "spooner."

Interest in milk glass waned around the First World War but returned stronger than ever late in the 1930s, when revived interest in Victorian glass inspired manufacturers to dust off their molds. Tableware lines were expanded to include dozens of items ranging from punch bowls to bread plates. Large-scale production continued through the late 1970s. Among the most prolific firms were the Imperial Glass Co. of Bellaire, Ohio, and the Westmoreland Glass Co. of Grapeville, Pennsylvania.

Today collectors can find vintage milk glass in abundance at flea markets and in antique shops. What's more, new designs are being offered by a growing number of firms. Among the factors that have made these pieces a hit with generations of collectors are durability, range of patterns from simple to ornate, and a unifying tone that works in just about any setting.

Prices range from a few dollars to more than $1,000, with rarity of design being one of the main factors affecting value.

Decorate with Spontaneity

If you are going to live with it, you've got to love it.

Balance new furnishings with flea-market finds to turn any room into a country retreat.

When mixing and matching periods and decorating styles stick to the following rules:

Comfort comes first—nothing in your home should be too precious to touch, use, or enjoy.

Mercury glass, green McCoy pottery, and an old painted portrait enhance a white, slip-covered collection of easy couches and living room chairs.

CAKE STANDS

Three hundred years after they first appeared on American tables, footed serving plates show no sign of stepping out of the spotlight. In 18th century America, dining à la française was all the rage, and accomplished hostesses were expected to present their guests with a feast for the eye as well as the palate. During the dessert course—envisioned as the sweet finale to a lengthy, multiple-course meal—tables were laden with lavish spreads of fresh, dried, and candied fruits, nuts, and sweetmeats, cakes and tarts, puddings and trifles, and syllabub and jewel-toned fruit jellies. Footed servers, known as salvers, would be stacked into pyramids at the center of the table and topped with an array of delicacies and decorations.

While dining in America has evolved into a much more casual affair, the practice of placing desserts on salvers—better known today as cake stands—has passed from generation to generation. From the ironstone and pressed-glass stands churned out by Victorian factories to the "Elegant Glass" serving pieces marketed by companies like Fostoria and Heisey during the Depression era, cake stands remain appreciated as much for their graceful form as for their utility.

Antique cake stands are still available through glass and ceramics dealers. Prices vary widely, with many pieces selling for less than $200.

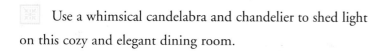 Use a whimsical candelabra and chandelier to shed light on this cozy and elegant dining room.

 Find French folding chairs to pull up to a sturdy dining room table.

Choose colors that work for you—for many, white is magical—it is uplifting, calming, and relaxing, and it works with almost everything you put with it.

FEATHER TREES

These relics from Christmases past are admired today for their homespun appeal. German immigrants brought many holiday traditions to our shores, among them, the feather tree. Crafted from wire frames and dyed goose feathers, the pieces became popular in Germany late in the 1800s, when efforts to save woodlands led to the widespread use of artificial Christmas trees.

It was President Theodore Roosevelt who sparked interest in feather trees in the United States. An avid conservationist, Roosevelt campaigned against felling live evergreens for Christmas trees, and in no time, retailers added feather trees from six inches to eight feet tall to their holiday offerings.

By the 1950s, feather trees had been replaced by artificial evergreens made from crepe paper and synthetic materials. Today both tabletop and room-size examples of feather trees are once again in demand.

Period trees from Germany, Japan, and the United States are rare and cost about $50 to $100 per foot.

FRESH AIR

Early Adirondack camps were built for pleasure and outdoor recreation. During their summer-long escapes from the industrial cities, visitors expected to spend much of their day exploring the forest with a native guide or navigating the lakes and streams in canoes and sailboats.

So go ahead and hang a hammock—suddenly you're on vacation in your own backyard.

Use restraint—surround yourself with collections of things that you find delightful and useful and leave the rest behind.

When renovating or decorating, be sure to save or replace elements that give a house its architectural identity—keep the original woodwork, windows, floors, fixtures, and cabinetry whenever possible.

White for others may be a disaster, especially if children are sharing the space. Go with darker colors and patterns to help blend in the wear and tear.

Vintage plank-seat chairs make good companions for a chunky dining table.

A floral hooked rug adds the right splashes of color to the white furniture.

Storage
Solutions

Match the size of the container to the items to be stored. Try to store efficiently and neatly by using jars, drawer or shelf dividers, bags, boxes, or baskets.

Figure out the role of each object: Can it be tucked away on a top shelf? Should something be wrapped in tissue paper and boxed for safekeeping? Does it need to remain within easy reach?

Built-ins are excellent. If you don't have them, then equip existing closets with ledges and pegs and add freestanding units such as drinking-glass containers and wine racks.

Hide things that need to be masked or protected.

Trunks, file boxes, baskets, and plastic containers are all good hidden storage options.

Form follows function—if you lack counter space consider hanging shelves instead.

Sideboards and armoires provide a great deal of accessible storage space inside and on top of the pieces.

You may already possess spaces and containers that are underutilized storage spaces in waiting. A length of peg board and some hooks can turn the inside of a door into a cleaning center with a place to hang a broom, a dust pan, a folding step stool, and cleaning rags.

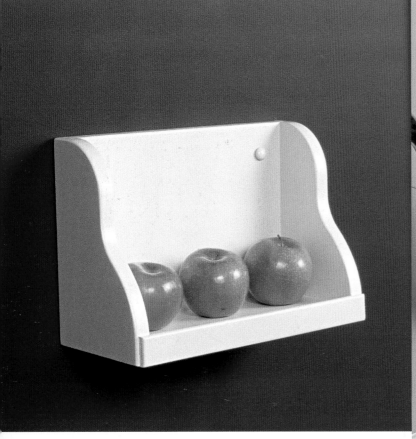

Identify Your Storage Needs. Define each "storage project" you want to tackle, such as organizing all the magazines that collect on top of your coffee table, or de-cluttering the kitchen drawers. The more specific you can be, the easier the project is to accomplish.

Things Most People Have and Can Probably Live Without

- Carry out menus

- Old phone books

- Games your family never plays (and/or games with missing pieces)

- Expired coupons

- Clothing that no longer fits

- Half-used and abandoned bottles of shampoo, lotion, and other toiletries

- Expired medicines

- Crushed or torn wrapping paper and ribbons

- Old catalogues

- Cans of dried out paint

- Duplicates of anything from blenders to blow dryers

Display items that are decorative as well as practical.

Sort your possessions according to their use. Figuring out how often you use things will determine where and how you need to store them.

Bookshelves, carts and shelving units are all portable pieces that give you both flexibility and freedom.

Condense your collections by getting rid of extraneous clutter.

Transform a wooden shipping crate into an all-in-one end table, portable bookshelf, and serving cart with a coat of paint and wheels.

PAINTED BASKETS

No one knows who first painted a basket, but whoever did so started a long-standing tradition. Particularly prized among collectors today are American splint baskets from the 1800s, which were crafted both by European settlers and Native Americans. Practical splint baskets quickly became farm standbys. These sturdy yet delicate works, usually woven from strips of ash or oak, were used for harvesting fruits and vegetables, gathering eggs, and an endless variety of other chores. Farmers probably painted them with whatever they had left over from other projects—homemade oil, milk, or factory-mixed paint. Popular colors included varying shades of red and robin's-egg blue. Paint preserved a basket both by protecting the surface and holding together the weave. It also served a more obvious purpose—to enliven homes and bring color into people's lives. That's what folk art is all about.

▨ Among the splint-wood offerings available today are rare 19th-century antiques with original paint, modern-day replicas woven by hand, and commercial painted baskets.

▨ Antique baskets in good condition are rare; those with original paint are most valuable. Expect to pay between $200 and $2,000 for a painted piece from the 1800s, often available through dealers specializing in 19th-century American antiques and folk art.

THE WATERING CAN

Long a workhorse of the garden, the watering can has been invited indoors. Large designs display fresh-cut flowers, diminutive pieces hold paintbrushes on worktables, and well-weathered forms stand alone as folk sculpture. No matter how you use them, these pieces look great in the house. Although watering cans have been made from copper, brass, iron, and aluminum in Europe and the United States for years, the classic two-gallon galvanized-steel designs with the extra-long spouts are most familiar today. Developed in Europe late in the 19th century, these cans were both lightweight and resistant to rust, thanks to a coating of zinc. Vintage examples are readily available on the market, while a growing number of manufacturers produce new designs with old-fashioned styling, ensuring the continued popularity of these classic garden tools.

Prices range from about $20 to $175 depending on such factors as age, material, and patina.

Make Rooms "Pop" on a Budget

Instead of spending lots of money on standout rare pieces, a white enamelware collection is given great prominence placed on a dining room sideboard, rather than in the kitchen.

A collection need not be comprised of the same objects grouped together; color can make that all-important connection among pieces.

Blur the lines between inside and outside: An Adirondack love seat, an old park bench and a group of early 20th century hand-made birdhouses provide a true country spirit to a living room.

A common color holds otherwise disparate pieces together. The interest is found in the various shapes and textures.

The magical thing about working against a backdrop of whites is that any bright object automatically becomes the center of attention.

Use texture wherever you can! Vary textures to increase the depth of a collection of white.

Use mirrors to introduce the beauty of reflected light.

An old, gold-lettered coffee can sets off flowers when used as a vase.

Blankets, bed linens, and other fabrics offer an endless source of variation and can be tossed over other furnishings to set a mood with little expense. Mix and match them on a bed, use them as throws over chairs and sofas, or just stack them up on a side chair.

It truly feels like country when soft accents right from your garden or grocer such as cabbage and pears, spruce up a white table while echoing the changing hues outside.

The ABCs of Wool

 Virgin wool is wool that has been spun only one time. It tends to be quite strong and less likely to pill than reprocessed wool, which is made of bits of recycled yarn that have been recarded and respun.

 Dyed-in-the wool refers to wool that is dyed before being spun; spinning more than one color together results in a heather yarn.

 Yarn-dyed wool is spun first then dyed, resulting in a solid color.

Wool is categorized by grades—fine, medium, and coarse—depending on the breed of sheep. Alpaca, merino, and Shetland—the finest grade wools—make the softest blankets.

Find the best place in your home to store textiles: Roomy closets, chests or cupboards in main living areas are recommended.

Basements and attics are prone to temperature and humidity fluctuations and are therefore unsuitable for storing textiles.

Be sure both the textiles and the storage area are clean before you start packing.

To prevent dust accumulation, wrap blankets in acid-free tissue or cotton sheets and stack them loosely.

Use moth deterrents—either traditional crystals or herbal sachets containing lavender or mugwort. Place these in a clean sock and lay it near, but not touching, the blankets.

Three or four times a year, shake out the textiles and inspect for insect infestation. Then vacuum the storage area, refold the blankets along different lines, and restack.

Cleaning Advice

New blankets can be hand-washed safely.

To test for colorfastness, place a few drops of water onto colored areas and press down firmly with a white blotter.

If no color appears on the blotter, place the blanket in a bathtub that has been filled with cold water mixed with a quarter cup of pH-balanced detergent.

Rinse well, roll between towels, and lay flat to dry.

Conservators should handle vintage textiles and those fabrics with colors that bleed. (Call your local historical society for referrals.)

Dry cleaning is not recommended for new or vintage blankets.

Create a Personalized and Organized Home Office

Flea-market finds such as a pine plank bench can serve as a fax machine station and a magazine rack.

Group a bunch of vintage (or new) wire baskets together for storing office supplies and knickknacks. The baskets can even display engravings and botanical prints.

Use wall space. Hold mementos in place on a ribbon board with vintage curtain pushpins.

Family rooms, kitchens, spare bedrooms, or any unused corner of your home can be claimed and turned into a functional communications area.

Recycle cast-off containers, hunt them down at flea markets, or buy new ones to hold documents, news clippings, and stationery supplies. Candy tins, wire baskets, and paper-covered bandboxes all make for great-looking storage.

Find a wooden tool carrier (or bring yours in from the garage!). Compartmentalize it with small garden pots to hold clips, pens, rubber bands and notes.

Mix old and new in your office space—it needn't be a sterile environment! Put up window shades made of vintage tablecloths.

PANTRY BOXES

Before America's kitchen shelves were filled with Mason jars, metal tins, cardboard boxes, and Tupperware, wooden boxes of all shapes and sizes were made to hold everything from spices and butter to cheese. Round or oval pantry boxes were first made locally by carpenters as far back as the 17th century and later mass-produced in 19th-century factories. "Some were simply varnished," says Yvonne Schlagheck, owner of StrawHorse Antiques in Temerance, Michigan. "But many were coated with milk paint or embellished with sponging or graining techniques." The Shakers perfected the craft, creating boxes revered by collectors for their skilled construction and fine finishes.

Today's homeowners have reclaimed these classic country pieces, using both antiques and reproductions for practical purposes (like storing receipts, stationery supplies, and sewing accessories) as well as for purely decorative displays.

Prices range from about $100 to $1,000 or more.

Tips for Great Country Kids' Rooms

▩ Toys and books tend to multiply in children's rooms so clever storage is important.

▩ Collections require prominent placement—school art projects and other handmade crafts deserve a place of honor. Use a sturdy painted plate rack to house hand-painted tableware.

▩ Pegs keep smocks within reach.

▩ Big glass jars serve as great containers for rocks, marbles, and seashells. Things stay neat and are displayed all at the same time.

Use transparent glass and plastic containers so that things can be easily identified.

Flea-market finds, such as a toy ironing board, can be covered and used as unexpected shelf space for books and games.

STEIFF TEDDY BEARS

Since the Middle Ages, bears have been brought to life by craftspeople and artists, and later in folklore, in children's books, and by toymakers. In 1883, German dressmaker Margarete Steiff began to sell soft-filled felt elephants, poodles, donkeys, and bears at her shop in Giengen, in Southern Germany, and the toys took off. Twenty years later, Richard Steiff, Margarete's nephew, designed a jointed mohair toy bear, which he introduced at Germany's Leipzig Spring Fair the following year.

Few other toys have the enduring appeal that the Steiff

teddy bear has. One look at their hand-stitched faces, sweet eyes, and soft coats, and collectors are hooked forever. The best materials and strict quality control is used in the making of these stuffed toys. They stand as gentle reminders of one's childhood and hold a respected place in toy history.

The success of Steiff bears, identifiable by their trade-marked Button in Ear, was so impressive that the company still refers to the period between 1903 and 1908 as the "boom years"—974,000 bears were made in 1907 alone. In 1910, Steiff bears could be purchased in 14 sizes. Today's collectors favor the traditional pre-First World War Steiff teddy bear with seams, lightly humped backs, elongated arms, well-defined feet, narrow ankles, and mohair plush. Their well-worn look is an added appeal for those collecting.

Most vintage Steiff bears were discarded when they could no longer be repaired; early examples in acceptable condition are hard to find.

Rare bears command high prices—a black mourning bear from 1912, known as the "Titanic Bear," recently sold at auction for about $145,000. Contemporary limited edition bears start at $150 and go as high as $700.

BLUE DENIM

Rugged, comfortable, and always at ease, blue denim is an American classic that gets even better with time. Through the years, California miners, cowboys, movie stars, trendy teens, and aging baby boomers have worn it. Today it also brings a relaxed feel to the home, thanks to throw pillows, bedding, table linens, and other accessories fashioned from the durable cotton fabric.

Denim has been produced in this country since the late in 18th century, but it was Bavarian-born business-man Levi Strauss who made it an American icon. In 1873, the San Francisco dry-goods merchant joined forces with Nevada tailor Jacob Davis, who came up with the ingenious idea of strengthening the pocket corners of pants with rivets. After receiving a patent for the process, the partners began producing copper-riveted "waist overalls" in blue denim.

Initially embraced by miners, farmers, and other manual laborers, blue jeans came to symbolize the swaggering American cowboy during the 1930s. In the 1950s they became all the rage for teens across the country after having been trotted out on the silver screen by Marlon Brando, James Dean, Annette Funicello, and Frankie Avalon. Later trends gave birth to bell-bottoms, designer jeans, and a craze for vintage denim that continues to this day.

❖ Prices of blue jeans can range from $25 to more than $10,000, depending on age, condition, and color.

❖ One collector paid $25,000 in 1997 for a rare pair of early Levi's discovered in an old coal mine.

❖ One-of-a-kind quilts have been fashioned out of well-worn jeans. These pieces can fetch $100 to $1,000.

A reconditioned locker basket chest can help organize the entire family with each member claiming a row of his own.

An old-fashioned general store-type bin or case can organize personal collections such as hair bands, purses, and ribbons.

Create a clothespin photo holder out of clothespins and wires. Kids will love the notion of swapping and adding newer pictures and art projects as they come into being.

GAME BOARDS

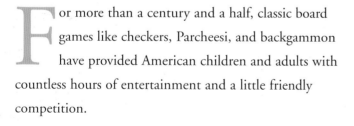

For more than a century and a half, classic board games like checkers, Parcheesi, and backgammon have provided American children and adults with countless hours of entertainment and a little friendly competition.

Today, antique wooden boards from the 19th and early 20th centuries—handcrafted by professional painters, signmakers, and home crafters—earn the admiration of folk art collectors who are drawn to their winning combinations of bold pattern and vibrant color.

A collection of 41 game boards, auctioned at Skinner, in Bolton, Massachusetts, this past February fetched prices ranging from $460 (for a turn-of-the-century, green-and-white painted checkerboard) to $46,000 (for a circa 1870 painted folding Parcheesi board).

Since antique examples are becoming more difficult to find, a variety of contemporary artisans replicate the game boards of the past. Prices range from $500 to $5,000, depending on age, rarity, graphic appeal, and patina.

Strike a Balance: A Cozy Cottage Space with Modern Conveniences

A dyed sisal rug and woven storage baskets add tactile interest to smooth painted floors.

Woven items balance smooth surfaces, such as solid surface counters, stainless steel appliances, and white painted wood-plank walls and floors.

Rooms with neutral colors get character from shocks of color in quilts, art, and flowers.

To make the most of available space, pay attention to detail. A narrow shelf holds toiletries and sits beneath a mirror and some framed folk art postcards. An empty bedroom corner is suddenly transformed into an extra dressing area.

In a small cottage with little closet space, alternative storage areas are essential. Low cabinets, armoires, trunks, and baskets fill the need for housing blankets, linens, and clothes.

Furniture and folk art help to ground the dreamy cottage in its rustic setting and its history. Folk pieces like American flags, tramp-art frames, and collections of antiques appear through the house.

CAMP BLANKETS

Established in Pendleton, Oregon, late in the 19th century, Pendleton Woolen Mills remains the foremost name in Indian trade blankets. Its first catalogue, published in 1901, pictured Chief Joseph (1840–1904) of the Nez Percé nation draped in a colorful Pendleton robe. The company produced more than 200 designs in the early 1900s under the three major brand names: Pendleton, Beaver State, and Cayuse.

While Native Americans prized Pendleton's warm woolen textiles, many American households preferred the easy upkeep and affordability of cotton. Founded in 1904, the Beacon Manufacturing Company became the nation's largest blanket maker, and it sold countless cotton bedcovers for less than $5 each through such outlets as J.C. Penney, Sears Roebuck, and Montgomery Ward. Department stores displayed the company's graphic blankets next to life-size images of Native Americans weaving traditional textiles.

Often called camp blankets today, these vintage textiles never lost their appeal as picnic blankets, bedspreads for weekend cottages, and knee-warmers at football games.

Collectors seek out vintage wool blankets by Pendleton, Capps, and other early-20th-centruy makers; cotton blankets from Beacon; as well as new blankets that possess an authentic feel.

There was a time when you could buy these blankets at a church bazaar or a flea market for less than $25, but those days are disappearing.

Antique Pendleton blankets range from $200 to $1,200, or more; cotton camp blankets start at less than $100, but rare designs can reach $900.

Antique quilts and a handmade basket adorn the walls and warm up a pared down living room.

Twig chairs, camp blankets, and quilts reinforce the Adirondack style.

In a small space, texture is a great design enhancer.

BLUE-AND-WHITE TRANSFERWARE

Intricate detailing and a timeless color combination have made this pottery a sentimental obsession for more than two centuries. Blue-and-white ceramics have captivated the Western world ever since Chinese porcelain first reached European shores. Early devotees included Queen Mary II, (ruler of England with William III, in the late 1600s, and

Augustus the Strong, king of Poland and elector of Saxony, who reportedly traded an entire regiment of soldiers for 48 Chinese vases. By the 18th century, millions of pieces of blue-and-white china were being shipped to Europe to satisfy demand.

The period from 1815 to 1835 is considered the golden age of blue-and-white transferware design because the color was intense and the patterns were delightfully diverse. Although the patterns became increasingly standard in the years following, the popularity of the color scheme endured. Introduced in the early 1900s, the Blue Willow pattern was sold through Woolworth's and Sears, Roebuck. The inexpensive wares became so common in Depression-era restaurants that they gave birth to the phrase "blue plate special."

Each transferware pattern began in the hands of an engraver, who painstakingly etched a design onto a copper printing plate. The printing plate was then "inked" with a cobalt-based color and used to make a print on tissue paper, which was, in turn, transferred onto a slip-glazed ceramic body. Only then was the piece ready to be fired.

Although the Chinese exports enjoyed immense popularity, English potters were the ones who put blue-and-white pottery on the tables of the masses. Printing methods developed in the mid-1700s allowed the detailed designs to be transferred rather than hand painted on pottery. The timesavings were immense, and factories in the Staffordshire region began churning out dinnerware and tea services decorated in blue and white. Favorite themes included scenic views of England, Italy, and India borrowed from popular travel books of the day. A variety of floral, fruit, and animal patterns also emerged, as did bucolic country scenes. Designs even catered to the American market by featuring patriotic images and such landmarks as the Erie Canal.

Antique prices for blue-and-white transferware range from about $50 for a simple, light-blue teacup or saucer to $2,000 or more for a platter or large pitcher that displays deep color saturation and a desirable pattern.

Give a Room a Seaside Cottage Feel

Use natural materials and neutral-toned textiles as the base for your floors, walls and furniture coverings. A tone-on-tone décor brings the calming influence of the beach indoors.

Display seashells and beachcombing mementos in collections.

Look for seashell-shaped vases and tiny oil paintings of ocean scenes.

Hang a group of small mirrors all with seashell frames on your wall.

Invigorate your neutral tones and white on whites with bursts of green—fill your deck or window boxes with white geraniums, succulents, and ivy.

Decorate a salvaged lampshade with touches of the seaside.

OLD GREEN GLASS

During the lean years of the 1930s, the best things in life were free, or at least remarkably inexpensive. The colorful molded-glass tableware that later became known as Depression glass was no exception. "The biggest event in my small town was the weekly 'dish night' at the movies," recalls Yeske, author of *Depression Glass: A Collector's Guide*. "After viewing a double feature for about 30 or 40 cents, a beautiful colored dish was handed to you." Similar promotional giveaways could also be found inside oatmeal boxes and sacks of flour, and individual pieces often sold for mere pennies at the five-and-dime.

How could vendors afford to sell or give away these sought-after products for practically nothing? They were mass-produced. Using the tank-molding process, the ingredients used to make glass—silica sand, soda ash, and limestone—were mixed and heated inside a ceramic tank. The molten glass then flowed through pipes into an automated pressing mold that churned out a seemingly endless variety of shapes and patterns. Although highly automated, there was an artistic side to the process. Someone had to design the pattern, and someone had to carve the mold. Lacy floral patterns like Cabbage Rose, Cherry Blossom, and Dogwood were popular, as were Art-Deco-inspired designs like Pyramid and Tea Room.

Antique Depression glass ranges from about $3.00 for a common saucer to more than $500 for a rare pitcher. Many pieces cost less than $50.

The Hand-Done Details

Create a dramatic backdrop for a bed by hanging velvet curtains on a rod from the wall. This also serves as a showcase for an old framed sketch.

A cachepot decorated with a hand-painted French interior scene provides an ornate little home for letters.

Each and every picture in a collection of landscape paintings and drawings tells a story. The detailed images give life to the room.

Pint-size landscapes dot a painted screen that works double duty concealing a corner for storage.

Very detailed European porcelains are grouped and displayed in a sweet cabinet.

The Perfect Bathroom

A bright, spacious, and restful room that is both practical and romantic—this bathroom opens up onto the garden. It is filled with classically inspired hardware as well as many small indulgences.

Exposed rafters, a galvanized potting table vanity, and many baskets—wicker and wirework—make a real connection with the outdoors.

Whites and neutral tones maintain the link with the outdoors and highlight the varied textures of the wood, tile, metal, stone, fabric, and fiber.

Fill a small wire basket with your favorite bath accessories and place it within easy reach of the tub or shower.

Vintage-style bath fixtures can soften the high-tech look of more modern luxuries such as a whirlpool tub.

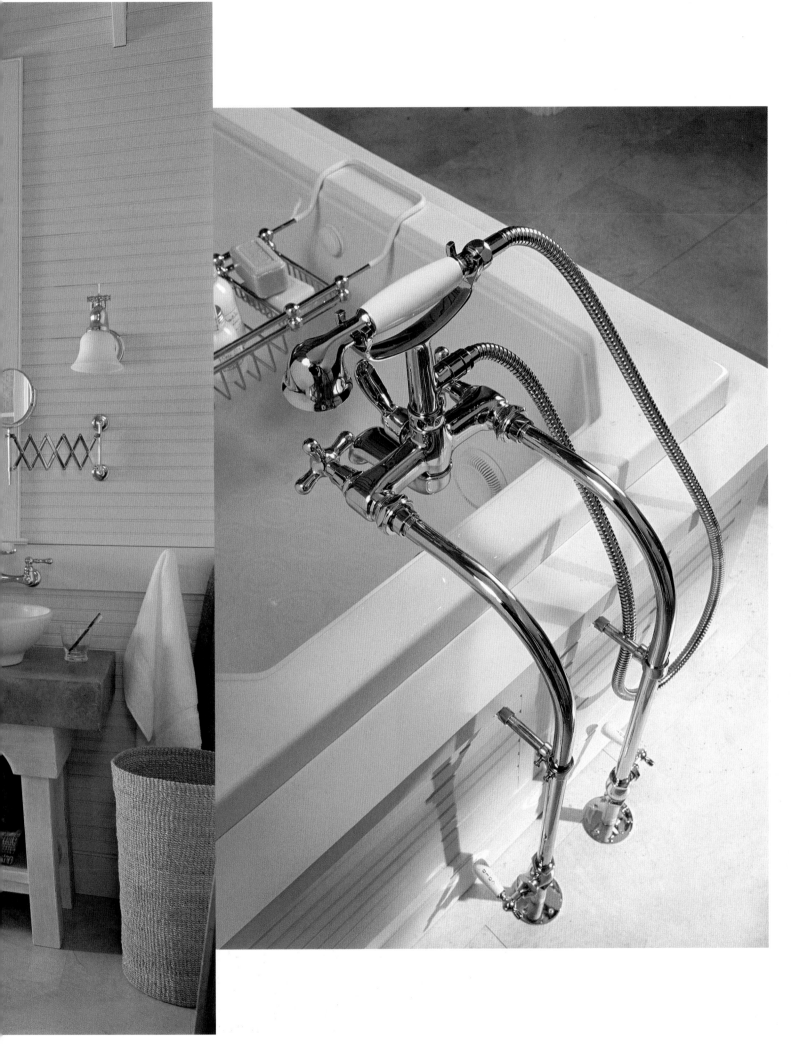

Three different widths of paneling—the narrow beaded-board walls, the tub surround, and the wide V-grove ceiling—add interest and flair.

Twin French doors open into the garden, evoking the simple spirit of a potting shed.

An antique cast-iron grate caps the fireplace.

Use chenille as an absorbent and comfortable covering for seat cushions.

ONE CHAIR

A single yet stylish piece—be it a chair, a table, even a lamp—can add the note of authenticity a room needs to take on a character all its own. Each single piece has a unique story to tell.

Use an armoire in the bathroom for stashing towels and linens, and to keep electronics out of the way. It can also display your collections.

Add a Twist of French Country Charm to Your Kitchen

Paint the walls a French blue and line them with pieces of vintage blue-and-white pottery.

An antique table and second-hand wicker chairs complete the eclectic kitchen nook.

Blue-and-white checks on the cushions add a real down-home country feel. Use leftover fabric to cover throw pillows for dashes of color.

Traditional diamond stencil on the pine floor adds authentic country charm.

Hand-painted tiles, a painted wooden headboard, and platters with floral designs adorn a well-proportioned hood. The modern stovetop disappears beneath the graceful curves of this decorative motif.

A butler's cabinet with its original brass pulls was put in the kitchen for storage.

A blackboard near the phone is a quirky and clever way to keep everything organized.

IRONSTONE PITCHERS

The pitcher is among the most practical household devices ever produced. In the second half of the 19th century, the pitcher of choice for many Americans was made of ironstone, a refined white earthenware produced by Staffordshire potteries in England. In 1813, English potter Charles Mason secured a patent for a new ceramic formula containing iron slag. Heralded as being more affordable and less subject to chipping and cracking than the porcelain, bone china, and creamware of the day, Mason's Patent Ironstone China enjoyed immediate success and was widely copied by English and American potters in the decades that followed. The wide array of forms produced included pitchers in all shapes and sizes, from diminutive creamers to large milk jugs and slender ewers.

Although English consumers favored pieces decorated with colorful Chinese- and Japanese-inspired motifs, Americans demonstrated a marked preference for the simplicity of plain white ironstone, so millions of gleaming white pieces were shipped to these shores.

White Granite, Paris White, Opaque Porcelain, and Pearl China are but a few of the enticing names English potteries used for their ironstone wares. Not all pieces were marked, however, making it difficult for beginning collectors to identify the real thing. In addition to seeking a maker's mark on the bottom of the pitcher, seasoned collectors also recognize ironstone by its color and weight.

White ironstone enjoyed its height of popularity in this country from the 1840s until the turn of the 20th century. Early pitcher designs showcased handsome Gothic forms, characterized by flattened hexagonal and octagonol panels.

The mid-1850s saw the rise in popularity of embossed patterns and naturalistic motifs—such as wheat, fruit, and foliage. Starkly simple designs, sometimes called "farmer's china," became popular in the 1870s and for some time later.

Whether holding a bouquet, kitchen utensils, or an ice-cold beverage, these hardworking wares are just as appealing as they were when they were first produced.

Period ironstone pitchers range from $75 for an unadorned creamer to $200 or more for a large decorative piece. Bargains still exist, however.

LITTLE
LUXURIES

Pamper guests with a tranquil bedroom furnished with a comfortable mattress and top-quality cotton bed linens that feel good against the skin.

Relax in an easy hammock for the afternoon.

Dress up a bed with floral sheets and pillowcases, ruffled shams, and a new white-work quilt trimmed with lace edges.

COUNTRY ICONS

GRANITEWARE

Bonnie Blue, Magnolia, Flint Grey, Ripe Concord Grape: The names once used to market American graniteware are as colorful as the pieces themselves. These durable enamel-coated goods have enlivened country kitchens since the late 1800s, when manufacturers began to churn out metal cookware and bakeware coated with mottled, swirled, and speckled designs.

First mass-produced in Europe, Graniteware took the country by storm at the end of the 19th century. Homemakers happily traded their lackluster cast-iron pots for items that were lively, lightweight, and easy to clean. By the early 1900s, some 80 companies nationwide were creating coffeepots, kettles, ladles, pitchers, pie plates, pudding pans, water pails, and sundry other goods, The variety of products was endless, and prices were low.

Antique Graniteware can range from $50 to $1,000 or more depending on rarity and age.

Collecting

Antiques

How to Display Your Collections

Don't be afraid to amass things you love.

Rely on similar colors to unify disparate objects.

Cluster kindred collectibles together to make a strong visual statement.

Avoid direct sunlight when displaying any collection. Vintage textiles, paintings, and photographs are especially susceptible to the bleaching effects of the sun's rays.

Find new uses for everyday items. For example, a mid-1800s lusterware pitcher finds new life as a vase. Other ideas include using apothecary bottles to hold toiletries in the bathroom, and jelly jars to store dry goods in the kitchen.

Some collectors insist that the thrill of the hunt is everything. For others, it's just the beginning.

Removing objects from their traditional context permits us to view them in a new light, but it also provides us with the challenge of discovering innovative ways to show the pieces to their best advantage.

BROWN-AND-WHITE TRANSFERWARE

The late-1800s Aesthetic Movement was the Golden Age of brown-and-white transferware's popularity," says Judith Siddall, owner of Merlin Antiques, in Palo Alto, Calif. "The earthy shades lent to the movement's 'back-to-nature' philosophy." In the century that followed, brown transfer-printed pottery was frequently bypassed by collectors who only had eyes for blue. But the past decade has seen trends shift again, with the rich, subtle hues of brown-and-white transferware gaining an ever-growing band of admirers. That such a renaissance would come about, collectors who favor brown might say, was only natural.

Transfer-printed tableware made its debut in England in the mid-1700s, when potters developed a method for using tissue paper to transfer detailed designs from inked hand-engraved copperplates to white-and cream-bodied pottery. The technique allowed entire sets of matching dinner plates, pitchers, tureens, tea services, and other pieces to be mass-produced and sold at prices affordable to America's middle classes. Wonderfully patterned, richly colored dinnerware soon appeared in kitchens throughout the country—not just on dining tables of those wealthy enough to afford hand-painted wares.

Among collectors, blue-and-white transfer-printed pottery has long remained a sentimental favorite—in part because of its intentional resemblance to early Chinese export pottery and in part owing to its sheer prolificacy: cobalt blue was the only color transferware that makers produced for decades. In the 1820s and '30s, however, potteries began to master other colors, including various shades of red, purple, green, and, naturally, brown.

Down-to-earth browns have had spurts of star power, enjoying a steady ascension into the limelight in recent years. Brown has really gained momentum as a collectible.

Rarity and condition affect value, as does the crispness of the color and the pattern.

Brown-and-white transferware's affordability compared to blue-and-white pieces has helped fuel the current wave of popularity. However, prices are rising steadily.

Plates with patterns reminiscent of the Aesthetic Movement range from $10 to $35, while early Staffordshire plates run $75 to $175 and up. An early four-piece soup tureen (including tureen, cover, ladle, and undertray) can average from $1,200 to $1,600.

Some of the most visually appealing arrangements place utilitarian objects of any vintage—quilts or teacups, cookie cutters or river rocks—against a neutral backdrop, where they can be appreciated for their sculptural qualities.

Displaying objects in small groups according to form, function, medium, or color helps to create a sense of cohesiveness.

Consider dividing an unwieldy collection of dinnerware and serving pieces, for example, into well-organized subsets of bowls, casserole dishes, and teacups and saucers.

Play with the objects you love until you find a look that strikes your fancy. It is the art of display, after all, that gives us a chance to share our passion for collecting.

LAWN CHAIRS

Metal lawn chairs are sentimental favorites with many Americans, calling to mind images of Grandma's garden and children at play on the well-groomed lawns of the 1950s. The chairs enjoyed their heyday after World War II, as legions of GI's returned home, tied the knot, and procured their own patches of green lawn in the suburbs. With the nation at peace, manufacturers churned out colorful tubular-steel-frame furniture that was fun, affordable, and easily transported from the patio to the picnic table.

Today these sturdy relics are eagerly collected. Some collectors repaint them in vivid hues, while others appreciate the worn look of a piece that has survived many seasons outdoors.

Vintage metal lawn chairs carry a price tag of $45 to $175 at flea markets or antique shops where dealers are well aware of their demand. Bargains, however, may still be found at tag sales or junk shops.

Everything You Need to Know About Country Auctions

Sometimes you don't have to have a particular object in mind when going to an auction. Scan the room for pieces that typify a particular style that you like.

If you are looking for an item to fit a specific place in your house, bring room dimensions and a tape measure with you.

Take along a magnifying glass, pad, pencil, and price guide.

Since sales at auctions are generally "as is" it is important to be able to closely view the pieces before you bid. Attend previews if you can. You will be able to inspect each lot—or items—to be sold.

Inspect the piece to judge its overall condition. Then pay attention to details: check joints, surfaces, pulls, and other elements.

Ask auction representatives questions—how old is it? Are all the parts original? Is there any damage?

Use a price guide to help you set a ceiling for your bidding. This is helpful in preventing you from paying too much if you get into a bidding war. You will have a preset idea about how high you want to go.

On the day of the auction, arrive early, register with the cashier and get your bidding card. Ask about fees—sometimes auctions add a buyer's premium of up to 15 percent to a winning bid.

Inquire about payment policies, shipping terms, and storage facilities.

Try to find a seat in the center rows where you can get a clear view of the auctioneer and the platform showcasing the lots. If none are available in the center, move to the back of the room where you are still in the auctioneer's line of vision.

When a lot you are interested in comes on the block, catch the auctioneer's attention by raising your bidding card. Don't wait until the end to jump in with an offer—you may miss out.

Bidding increments are usually $25, but when the bidding slows down, the auctioneer may accept another amount.

 If you are only interested in one object or are on a tight schedule, ask the auctioneer when a particular lot is likely to come up.

 If you are not able to attend an auction, register an absentee bid while at the preview. This will indicate the highest price you will pay for an item.

If you plan to transport your purchase by car or truck yourself, take along bubble wrap, newspaper, old blankets, and rope. For a fee, auction companies will arrange for delivery for larger items.

After the auction, if an item you were interested in did not sell, inquire whether it had a reserve. A reserve price is set by the seller, and it is the lowest price for which the item may be sold. You may be able to purchase it for the reserve amount or less.

PICKUP TRUCKS

Driving an antique pickup allows you to be both stylish and practical. Originally made to serve farmers, laborers, and factories, antique pickup trucks embody the notion that America was built on hard work. One of the first pickup trucks, which rolled out of a Chicago shop in 1896, was nothing more than a motorized wagon. Though designs quickly improved, they failed to gain traction with the public. Then in 1917, Dodge realized that the light-utility trucks it was selling to the U.S. Army might appeal to civilians. Dodge's new pickup was a hit, and close to 30,000 had sold by the end of 1920. Before long, Ford, Chevrolet, International, and other makers were churning out competitors.

For years pickups remained working vehicles: During the 1930s, the sight of overloaded farm trucks heading West to escape the Dust Bowl was a constant reminder of rural poverty. Since the Second World War, however, pickups have attracted a broader following, appealing equally to country farmers and urban professionals, for work and for play. Last year, automakers sold about 3.2 million new pickups in the United States, outpacing popular family sedans like the Ford Taurus.

Most collectors' groups define an "antique" pickup as any model older than 30 years (as opposed to a "classic," which can be as recent as 10 years).

Prices for functioning trucks range from $1,000 to $30,000. Condition and scarcity affect price.

Collectors generally buy from individuals, not dealers, so begin by contacting major historic truck organizations or by looking at publications aimed at antique truck buyers.

Family Pictures— Caring for Your Collections

The biggest threat to photographs in the home is direct exposure to sunlight.

In order to reduce the threat of overexposure, be sure to frame your photographs with glass or Plexiglas that has a layer of UV protection.

When it comes to displaying them, select walls or table-tops that are out of direct sunlight. Once or twice a year, rotate displays, varying the amount of light that each photograph is exposed to.

Turn an unexpected place into a showcase for your collection—use the space along the staircase for hanging photographs.

Photo albums with rag-paper pages and photo corners are actually the most archivally sound.

Another source of damage stems from the actual albums used to store photographs. Albums from the 1960s through the 1980s utilized paper, plastic, and adhesive that were all highly acidic. Chemicals from the album materials will seep into the photographs themselves, causing discoloration and brittleness.

Conservation-supply catalogues and art stores are good bets for reliable materials.

When shopping for new albums, look for examples that have pages and adhesives purported to be archival, acid-free, non-acidic, or museum-quality.

Unless a photograph is in complete darkness, there will always be some exposure to harmful ultraviolet rays, whether the piece hangs near a natural light source or an artificial one.

If you chose an album with plain paper pages, be sure to avoid nonarchival adhesive tape and glue when attaching photographs.

Opt for acid-free paste or photo corners, which can be found in black, white, or clear in plain or decorative designs.

Before you store photographs, write down biographical information about each of the subjects. Future generations will thank you.

Photographs not being framed or placed in an album should be laid flat in sturdy archival boxes. For extra protection, layer acid-free tissue or museum-quality mat board between the images.

Steer clear of attics or basements when storing photograph-filled boxes, since the temperature and humidity fluctuations can cause serious damage.

Closets or cupboards located on the main floor of your house are good places to store albums and archival boxes.

Keep photographs and archival boxes in an environment that best duplicates the temperature and humidity levels under which you feel most comfortable.

Surface damages, including scratches, tears, and stains can usually be corrected by photo conservators.

Digital-imaging systems can retouch vintage photographs and duplicate one-of-a-kind images.

Bauer Ware

In the late 19th century, in Paducah, Kentucky, J. Andy Bauer purchased a pottery factory to produce utilitarian wares such as stoneware crocks, pitchers, and jugs. It was, however, the second factory he opened in the outskirts of Los Angeles in 1910 that turned out the pottery that is avidly collected today.

Bauer's most recognizable pieces, designed by Louis Ipsen after Andy Bauer's death, is Ring-Ware which is so-named for its ringed or "ruffled" pattern of concentric circles.

Ring-Ware brought glossy and vibrant shades of blue, green, orange, yellow, red, and black to tables that had long seen only white. As any Bauer collector can attest, color, style, and condition are critical.

When first produced, a set of five bowls sold for less than $2.00, and a pitcher or teapot could be purchased for $1.00.

Today, prices vary widely because many dealers and collectors are unsure of the availability of certain forms.

As Bauer pottery becomes more popular with collectors, prices are rising, and certain patterns in specific colors can sell for hundreds of dollars apiece. Teapots, water pitchers, mixing bowl sets, and cookie jars are in high demand, and are therefore quite pricey.

Hanging Match Holders & Chocolate Molds

⁂ Until the invention of the sulfur-tipped friction match early in the 1800s, starting a fire in an open hearth was a chore. Homemakers and kitchen workers had to rely on tin-derboxes containing flint and steel, which, when struck together, produced a spark.

⁂ Matches not only saved time but also proved eminently safer than struggling with a tinderbox in a dark, unheated house.

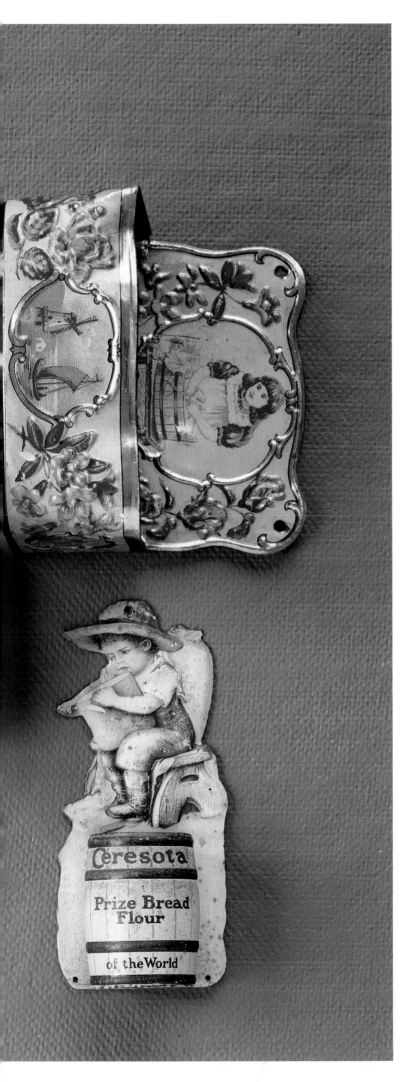

As the new devices became readily available, they created their own necessity: A protected, dry storage place that was both within easy reach of those who needed to use them and away from curious children and the occasional midnight mouse.

Although shelves and tabletops were convenient resting places, many people hung handmade or manufactured holders beside the fireplace or stove.

The 1873 catalogue of one British firm took pains to explain the benefits of such containers: "The Patent Safety Match Holder is intended to be nailed up to prevent it being carried around the house, thus saving much loss of time, as it frequently happens that boxes that are not fixed are carried into other rooms, and when it is really of importance to obtain a light quickly, cannot be found."

The first hanging match holders were often carved from wood, either by a homeowner or a local craftsperson. Many of these early holders were crudely constructed and had limited ornamentation. Pieces crafted by tinsmiths commonly bore painted or inscribed motifs, enlivening the surfaces. Whether simple or ornate, a standard form emerged that changed little over time: a pocket or box to hold the matches and an abrasive surface on which to strike them. Some holders also featured trays for spent matches.

Match holders held their place in American kitchens well into the 20th century, but the advent of electric ranges and gas stoves with pilot lights obviated the necessity of keeping matches near the stove in most kitchens. By 1950, production of match holders had all but ceased. Many were thrown away while others were relegated to attics or basements.

Match holders are now sparking the interest of collectors, who will most likely find vintage match holders at antiques shows, flea markets, garage sales, and country auctions, especially those that feature kitchenware.

Prices range from about $50 to $250, depending on age, rarity, and condition.

Although most examples were rarely dated, some do bear a patent date on the back, enabling a collector to identify the exact production period. Serious collectors also check for the registered numbers or marks that can be traced in the U.S. Patent Index or similar published sources.

Period trade and mail-order catalogues can also be helpful in identifying the dates and manufacturers of various holders.

Collecting Vintage Hats

Vintage hats reveal a bit of the personalities of their previous owners.

Collecting vintage hats provides for a woman a way to make a real personal connection to the past.

Self-expression is a big draw for today's hat collectors as well. Many collecotrs buy old hats to wear, while others use them to decorate their homes.

No matter what purpose you have in mind, you can find old hats in vintage-clothing stores and at flea markets, estate sales, and country auctions.

Boxed hats in pristine condition are easier to find in rural and suburban areas because storage was not as much of an issue in country houses as it was in city apartments.

Most early-to mid-20th century hats sell for about $20 to $125 depending on condition, materials, and intricacy of construction

Unusual styles and designer creations can sell for several hundreds of dollars apiece.

Valuable or delicate hats should be handled with extra care: Store them in hatboxes supported on all sides by acid-free tissue and rotate displays every few months to lessen exposure to sunlight and dust.

Chocolate molds were in full production from 1880 to 1940. It was after the Second World War that the handmade craft of candy making gave way to the relative ease and low expense of mass production. Today, these whimsical artifacts of yesterday's candy kitchen continue to delight collectors.

Manufacturers in Europe and the United States produced detailed molds made of tin, pewter, and copper. The stamped metal bunnies, sheep, turkeys, dogs, cats, hearts, eggs, Santas, and other motifs were intended both for commercial bakeries and individual homes.

Detailing is one of the major factors affecting the value of a piece. Small molds with limited detail, for example, can still be found between $10 and $25.

More desirable pieces featuring extremely fine blades of grass, strands of hair, creases in clothing, or other decorative elements sell for up to $100 or more.

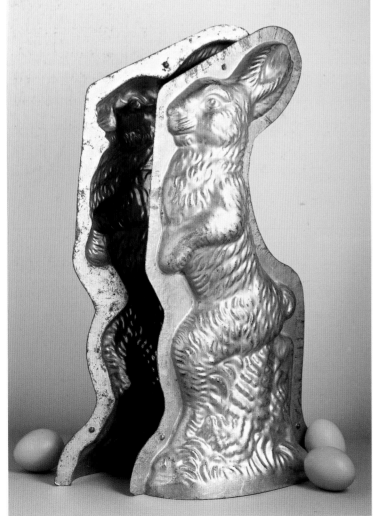

Size is another important factor that can affect the value of a chocolate mold. The smallest molds that collectors will encounter stand three to five inches tall, and the most common examples range from six to 12 inches in height.

Larger molds range from 15 to 20 inches in height while the rarest, tallest examples top off at two to three feet. Molds of this size have sold for as much as $5,000.

The best places to search for vintage chocolate molds include antique shops (especially those specializing in kitchenware), holiday collectible fairs, and flea markets.

When inspecting a stamped-tin mold, look closely to see whether it has all its companion parts—including clamps, straps, and clips.

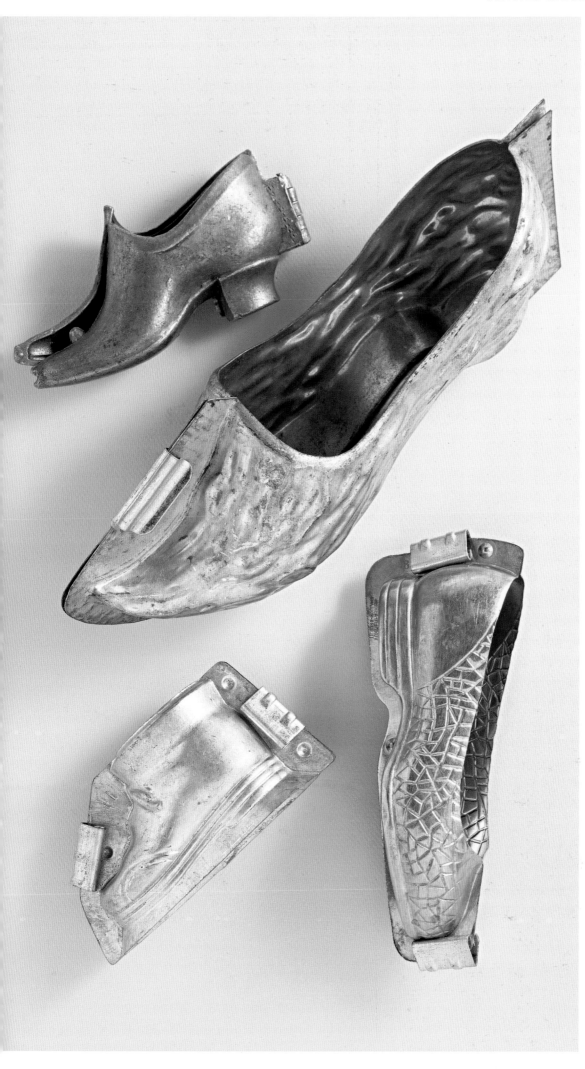

Reproductions do exist, but they generally stand out when compared to authentic pieces: Vintage examples tend to be made of heavy-gauge tin, boast greater attention to detail, and possess their share of small nicks and dents consistent with repeated use.

Chocolate molds make an eye-catching display on shelves, sideboards, and mantels, but are not just for show. As it turns out, many of these collectors are cooking and kitchenware enthusiasts who use the molds to create old-fashioned confections.

THE MORE THE MERRIER

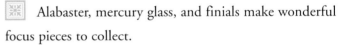

◼ Alabaster, mercury glass, and finials make wonderful focus pieces to collect.

◼ Alabaster is an opalescent marble-like stone; mercury glass sandwiches a silvery substance between twinned glass molds.

◼ The Victorians loved both, especially in the form of urns, vases, candlesticks, and spheres.

◼ Wooden spherical finials, destined for curtain poles, look handsome in a group.

When collecting, go by gut and love; if you like something, don't be afraid to try it out. Always ask yourself, "How would three or more look together?" And keep going until it feels right.

T.S.& T. Lu-Ray Pastels

Lu-Ray Pastels were introduced in 1938 by the Ohio firm Taylor, Smith & Taylor Co. (T.S.&T.). The company marketed Lu-Ray as an alternative to the bold "fiesta" colors then popular in "modern" dinnerware. More than a half century later, the Art Deco–inspired plates, platters, pitchers, tumblers, and teacups still catch collectors' eyes.

These pieces were originally produced in four colors: Windsor Blue, Sharon Pink, Surf Green, and a buttery yellow called Persian Cream. A fifth color, Chatham Gray, was added to the line in 1949 but didn't prove as popular with homemakers as the original four. Chatham Gray was discontinued in 1955. The rarity of pieces in this color has made them quite desirable among today's collectors.

The line's immediate success encouraged the manufacturer to add new pieces every year through 1942, including a tiny bud vase and urn in 1939, a covered muffin plate in 1940, a set of four nesting mixing bowls in 1941. Lu-Ray Pastels remained one of America's most popular dinnerware patterns through the early 1960s (production ceased in 1961). After that time, piles of the colorful pieces were discarded, often viewed simply as unfashionable "old dishes." This unfortunate turn, coupled with 60 years of repeated use and the inevitable breakage, has dramatically decreased the supply of Lu-Ray. Because of the pattern's revived popularity with collectors over the past few years, the hunt for quality Lu-Ray Pastels—especially certain rare designs—has become more challenging.

For those collectors who savor a seek-and-find mission, there is still plenty of Lu-Ray to be found.

Common pieces can be found for $10 to $15, and rare pieces even appear from time to time in unexpected places, but those can often cost $100 to $200.

The Layered Look

❋   Layering tone upon tone creates a peaceful ambiance in a room.

❋   Ten different fabrics and textures can be used in combination, yet the result is soothing—not "busy."

❋   Damasks, stripes, and eyelet echo one another in intensity and scale.

❋   Try layering rag rugs on top of your carpet.

Darners

There was a time when no proper household was without at least one of these sewing tools. Stocking darners came in myriad sizes, shapes, materials, and colors, but each one had the same function—to keep fabric taut while being darned.

Also known as darning balls, eggs, spools, bells or mushrooms, these mending tools were most popular during the time people believed in using something up, wearing it out, making do, or else doing without!

The proliferation of a more disposable society saw little need for this tool, but a new interest has emerged in the darner as a highly sought after collectible.

A 19th-century teacher instruction manual espouses darning as part of the American public-school curriculum: "Wisely taught, it develops the thrifty dispositions and habits of neatness, cleanliness, order, management, and industry."

Darners were made from almost every imaginable material, most commonly wood, as well as stag horn, mother-of-pearl, ceramic, porcelain, celluloid, plastic, Bakelite, papier-mâché, aluminum, ivory, brass, and tin.

Many of the glass darners were not always intended to be used but to showcase the artisan glassblowers' talents.

Darners ranged in size from $1/2$-inch miniatures to nine-inch-long mushrooms with $4^1/2$-inch-wide caps.

A flea market search might find wooden darners for less than $10. A more unique piece, such as an art-glass darner, was sold at auction for $1,000.

Vintage Syrup Pitchers

Hot cakes, pancakes, griddle cakes—whatever you call them, these are true country breakfast fare. The name may vary regionally, but just about everyone likes to smother them in sweet maple syrup. Over the years, serving up these scrumptious flapjacks has led to the design of some beautiful and innovative pitchers, objects that are prime for collections.

The history of the syrup pitcher begins in the mid-19th century, when the Victorian way for ornamentation and strict etiquette codes ruled the day.

Maple syrup pitchers, previously utilitarian earthenware or tinware pitchers and jugs, were crafted from ironstone (for the more casual meal), and silver-plate and pressed glass (for formal breakfast tables).

The late 1800s saw the first silver-plate pitchers with embossed botanical images, with matching plates or small trays, as well as decorative lids.

Typically, embossed syrups as some collectors refer to them, were fitted with pewter lids and thumb catches while plain ironstone ones had slide-on lids made from tin.

More striking designs came about with the advent of pressed glass, milk glass, etched glass, and art glass both in the U.S. and abroad.

Eventually, the need arose for everyday dishware that was well suited to the wear-and-tear of the average kitchen. By the turn of the century, syrup pitchers were being made from enamelware. American manufacturers produced upright pitchers with metal lids in marbled or mottled patterns. European companies emblazoned them with checked, striped, and floral designs.

The variety of materials and shapes used in the 20th century to create pitchers was vast. These included inexpensive colored glass pitchers with glass or hinged metal lids, sometimes fitted with matching saucers or underliners, as well as clear glass with Bakelite lids or tin lids with Bakelite handles.

Inexpensive crystal and clear-glass pourers with chrome and plastic lids and handles have been produced since the 1930s.

Stores that specialize in vintage kitchenware are the best resource for finding these collectibles. Depression-glass pieces are more common than those from the 1800s because of their mass production.

The fancier Victorian pitchers are valued according to their condition, rarity, and size. Embossed ironstone pitchers may be $200 to $300; silver-plate and glass syrup pitchers start at $100; while plain ones sell for about $75.

Flea markets and garage sales are where you will find many of the pitchers from the 1950s and 1960s, with bright-colored plastic lids and handles.

The enamelware pieces can cost $40 to $60; more elaborate examples with rare patterns can be had for upward of $350.

Depression glass sells for about $40 to $80, while rare colors and patterns might be $200. The clear-glass pitchers with chrome or plastic lids can still be found for $8 to $15.

PAINT BY NUMBERS

This once popular dime-store hobby has captured the imagination of millions as a true American collectible. Today, more than 50 years after its introduction, paint by numbers has become a real embedded icon of popular culture.

Numbered paint sets for children date back to the 1920s, but it was at the 1951 New York Toy Fair that this craft activity became known.

Dan Robbins, head of the art department at Detroit's Palmer Paint Co., was inspired by Leonardo da Vinci's reported practice of assigning numbered sections of his paintings to his apprentices. Robbins believed that this was a great way for hobbyists to learn how to paint. He proposed the idea to Palmer Paints who then marketed it worldwide.

After a few years, at least 35 other companies were selling paint by number kits.

Millions of adults and children were painting, using little paint pots and prenumbered surfaces. Companies such as Craftint, Art Award, Picture Craft, and Palmer Paint's Craft Master deluged the postwar leisure market with these pre-patterned pictures.

The kits sold for $2.50 apiece, and included 3 unpainted images, two brushes, thinner, and a palette of colors. The technique was so well received that during President Eisenhower's first term in 1954, a gallery of paint by numbers was installed in the West Wing of the White House.

In the 1960s the craze faded, but today is reemerging as a collectible that represents a very specific time in American culture. This art-in-a-box gave, and continues to give those not artistically inclined a chance to experience art. It embodies the post-War mechanization of culture.

Today's collectors are drawn to paint by numbers because of the nostalgia the images evoke and because they are historic pieces of folk art. These treasures can be found in flea markets, thrift shops, yard sales, and the Internet for as little as $5.00 and upward of $350 for such reproductions as Leonardo's Mona Lisa.

Collectible Tablecloths

American kitchens from the late 1940s and '50s were filled with lively colors and bright patterns. Countertops, curtains, and floor treatments tended to echo the home-maker's passion for color, as did fresh looking tablecloths and napkins.

Textile companies such as Prints Charming, Wilendure, and Table Tempo produced enchanting colorful tablecloth designs.

Everyday tablecloths were mostly square, commonly 52 x 52 inches and 40 x 40 inches. Homemakers were able to buy a variety of table linens as they sold for about $2 a tablecloth in department stores.

The 1960s and 1970s saw a shift from floral, fruit, and graphic patterns toward a more modern feel with geometric shapes and earth tones. In addition, more women were working outside the home leaving little time for the cleaning and pressing these linens required. Therefore, stacks of these "old-fashioned" linens were stored away in attics, donated to Good Will or tossed out.

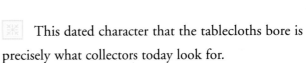

This dated character that the tablecloths bore is precisely what collectors today look for.

Customers who buy these linens do so because of the real sense of home and hearth the items relay. Many people see prints that perhaps bring back fond memories of their childhood.

Look in antique stores specializing in vintage kitchenware or period textiles.

A quality piece will range anywhere from $25 to $75, depending on its size, condition, rarity of design and color.

Complete sets—tablecloths with matching napkins—are more valuable, as well as those with original labels and gift boxes.

Real bargains can be found in flea markets and yard sales for as little as $5 to $15.

Caring for Vintage Table Linens

Soak the item overnight in cool water to remove the yellowing of age and discoloration along fold lines.

For gentle, allover whitening, add 1 cup of white vinegar to a washbasin or washing machine set on the delicate cycle.

The white vinegar also gets rid of the musty smell linens sometimes get from being stored in a damp basement.

A paste of white vinegar and salt makes an excellent spot remover.

Stretch the cloth while it is still damp and then press with a warm iron.

Crafting with Vintage Tablecloths

Don't pass up a great patterned or brightly colored tablecloth just because it has a spot on it or is slightly torn.

Use the fabric to make one-of-a-kind pillow covers.

Clothing such as sundresses and jackets can be fashioned from vintage tablecloths.

Find a selection of patterned and colored linens and make cushion covers for your dining room. There is no need to have them all matching—the fun is in the variety! (For additional projects see crafts on page 341.)

Will It Be Hot or Not? Tips for Predicting the New Collectibles

Was it produced in limited quantities? Items manufactured in small numbers are considered more desirable than mass-produced objects.

Have most people thrown it away? Items produced and collected with the intention of cashing in on their future value rarely appreciate.

Is the item an original and not a commemorative? Collectors tend to prefer authentic items, not reproductions produced for a special event or anniversary.

Was it made to last? Condition always affects value, so buy well-constructed pieces made from materials that do not deteriorate over time.

Does it have crossover appeal? Very often the highest prices are achieved for those antiques that appeal to collectors from more than one field of interest.

Was it available for only a short period? Items that were available for limited periods of time will be more desirable, as fewer people had the opportunity to obtain them.

Is it all the rage with kids today? Many people began collecting toys they played with in their youth when they are 30 and have disposable income for the first time. See what your 10-year-old is playing with now.

Was it hard to obtain? Premium merchandise that required mailing in a proof-of-purchase seal or coupon is generally produced in smaller numbers and is of higher quality than many items available in the stores.

Will it be obsolete? Computers, for instance, have made typewriters collectible. What objects in our daily lives might no longer be used 20 years from now?

Is it the first of many versions? When there are many versions produced of one object—whether it is a work of art, a book, or a toy—the earliest edition is generally the most desirable.

TRULY DREAMY ANTIQUES— DAYBEDS

▨ Daybeds are more intimate than a settee yet more formal than a bed.

▨ These timeless forms that merge comfort and style can be characterized as any kind of seating intended for daytime repose.

▨ Beginning with the ancient Greeks, many forms of daybeds evolved. All served a variety of roles, providing a place to sleep in a private bedchamber, to receive visitors in a formal salon, or even to dine beside a low table.

▨ Names for these chairs include the French chaise longue ("long chair"); the miridienne, a chairlike sofa with one arm higher than the other; and the ricamier—a backless bed.

▨ Country daybeds were made by rural cabinetmakers during the mid-19th century.

▨ In New England, a daybed with an out-turned back and incurved legs was known as a "hired man's bed." This served as a spare bed in an all-purpose room—which is very much how daybeds are used today.

▨ Many daybeds remain reasonably priced. An antique metal daybed can range anywhere from $500 to $4,000 and up.

VENICE
NANTUCKET
SIPADAN
CHESAPEAKE COUNTRY
GARDENS OF MEXICO
GARDENS IN PROVENCE
the house of the architect
Nantucket Island
SALGADO WORKERS APERTURE
HE SPLENDOR OF FRANCE
MEDITERRANEAN VERNACULAR

Collecting Quilts— Sorting through the Layers

Tumbling Blocks is a quilt pattern that is made up of hundreds of tiny fabric diamonds pieced to create a three-dimensional effect. Crib quilts and Amish examples featuring this design are especially popular with collectors. This pattern was popular with quilters in the early part of the 19th through the early 20th centuries.

Log Cabin Quilts are named for the narrow strips or "logs" of fabric pieced to form individual blocks. Altering the placement of light and dark strips creates variations on this pattern known as Courthouse Steps, Windmill Blades, and Barn Raising. Fine examples of these dating to the last quarter of the 19th century are quite costly in today's market. The more affordable quilts are those with wider logs (one-half to one inch in width).

Star Quilts are probably most popular with collectors. These motifs first appeared in the early 19th century and continued all the way through the 20th century. The smaller the stars, the more interest there is.

STAR QUILTS

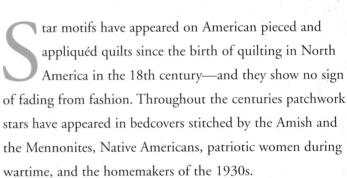

Star motifs have appeared on American pieced and appliquéd quilts since the birth of quilting in North America in the 18th century—and they show no sign of fading from fashion. Throughout the centuries patchwork stars have appeared in bedcovers stitched by the Amish and the Mennonites, Native Americans, patriotic women during wartime, and the homemakers of the 1930s.

Perhaps the most famous of all pieced patterns is the single eight-point star known as the Star of Bethlehem, or Lone Star, quilt. Formed from hundreds of meticulously cut and joined diamond-shaped patches, this demanding design's variations include Broken Star and Sunburst. Stars have always been a prominent element on patriotic quilts. Patriotic quilts and star quilts of all varieties have enjoyed a wave of renewed popularity in recent years.

WEDDING RING QUILTS

"Vogue for quilts has swept the country," The Missouri Ruralist declared on February 1, 1931. "One fair had 161 entries of the Wedding Ring design alone." Among the reasons this pattern enjoyed such popularity were the endless design opportunities it offered quilters, including pastel-on-white, solid-color backgrounds, two-tone rings, and fanciful borders. Craftspeople continue to interpret this beloved pattern today. Minnesota quilter and author Susan Stein has pieced more than 50 Wedding Ring designs, many embellished with appliqués, beadwork, and hand-painted details.

Few motifs in the quilter's lexicon are as recognizable as the interlocking rings of the Wedding Ring pattern. The distinctive design—whose full name, Double Wedding Ring, is commonly shortened by collectors and quilters—first appeared in the 1920s, when the United States witnessed a renewed interest in the furnishings and crafts of an earlier era. It wasn't until the 1930s and '40s, however, that the pattern reached its height of popularity, and countless variations were printed in newspapers and ladies' magazines. Because the rings were made of numerous snippets of fabric, a quilter could find the makings of a glorious textile in her scrap bag, a boon during the Depression and War years, when money was limited.

The pattern's most appealing aspect may have been its simple message of hope for the future. The wedding ring was a joyous symbol in what were otherwise hard times. Small wonder, then, that the pattern remained a favorite option for industrious brides-to-be as well as friends and relatives of betrothed couples searching for the ideal gift.

Wedding Ring quilts range in price from $300 to $3,000 depending on age, condition, quality of construction, and design.

Examples that display a colored background and those with six or more rings in a single row are especially prized.

Patriotic Quilts are probably the most sentimental of all designs as they were created during times of national celebration, Presidential elections, or troubling times. Red, white, and blue is the color scheme, and the most common motifs are American flags, eagles, and portraits of statesmen.

Baltimore Album is a design where each appliquéd block is more elaborate than the next. These quilts from about 1840 to 1860 can command a price tag of $10,000 or more.

Pictorial Quilts are most often appliquéd, featuring one motif repeated in rows to create an eye-catching overall pattern. The most popular subjects featured have been dogs, cats, birds, boots, baskets, and coffee cups. Some examples date from the early 19th century, however, more common are the kit quilts from the 1920s to the 1940s.

Schoolhouse is the best-loved repetitive pattern. This design was executed in the latter half of the 19th century. The huge popularity of vintage red-and-white and blue-and-white quilts, coupled with their rarity on the market, has spawned reproduction in recent years. Be careful and buy from someone well schooled in vintage textiles.

LOG CABIN QUILTS

Named for the slender strips of fabric, or "logs," used in their construction, Log Cabin quilts number among the most beloved textiles. Although no one knows the exact origins of the design, historians agree that American quilters adopted the pattern sometime during or immediately following the Civil War and quickly made it—along with the crazy quilt—one of the most popular pieced quilts of the late 19th century. At the center of each quilt is a square "hearth" or "chimney" (most often in red or black), around which the narrow fabric "logs" are pieced. But it takes more than sentimental feelings for a quilt pattern to remain popular for more than a century. Log Cabins also offered quilters a rare creative opportunity: Alterations in the placement of light and dark fabrics resulted in the endless design variations that continue to fascinate today's collectors and home decorators.

Crazy Quilts are late 19th century creations that are characterized by mismatched bits of jewel-toned silks, satins, and velvets, embellished with embroidery, paint, and ribbons.

Double Wedding Rings and Grandmother's Flower Garden are made up of small bits of fabric pieced together to create an overall effect of interlocking rings or hexagonal flower beds. These are most often associated with the pastel colors to the Depression-era quilts.

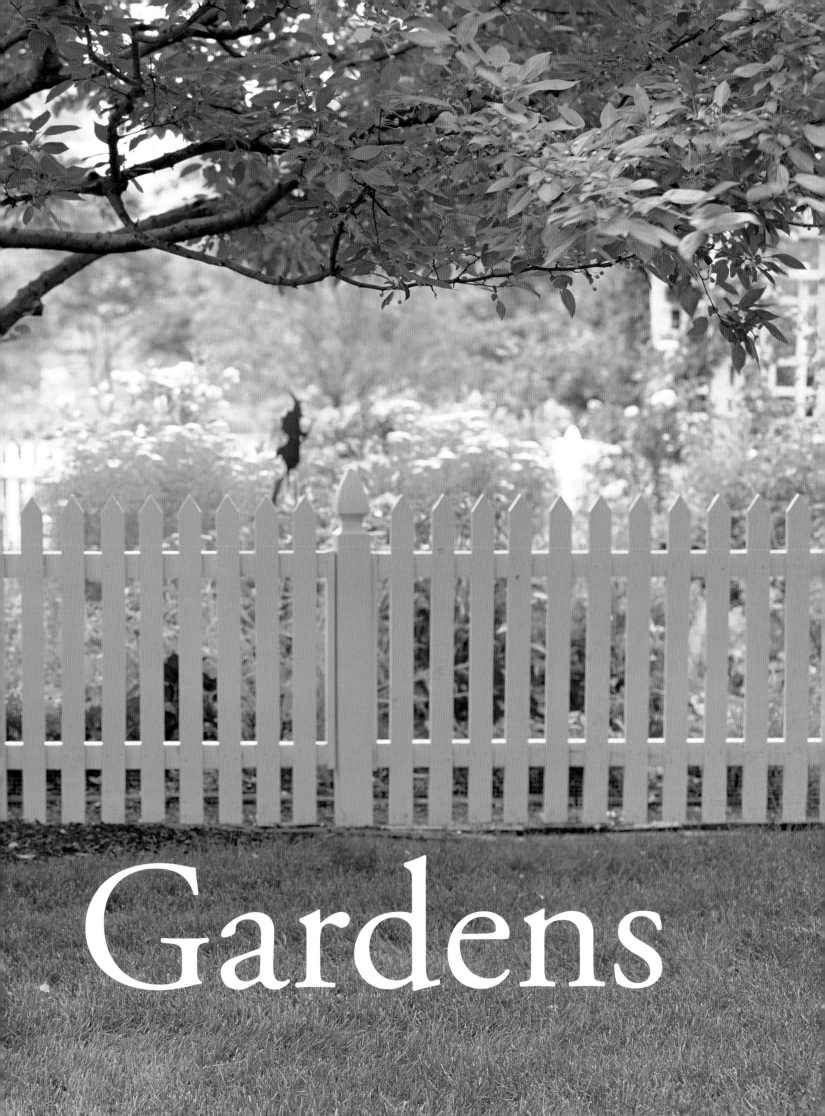

Gardens

The Right Fence

The main purpose of any fencing should be to visually define borders or limits of a particular area in a landscape while remaining an integral part of it. The fence needs to encompass the space clearly while relating cohesively to the entire landscape and, to the architecture. It requires both a logical starting place and a sensible finishing point. When choosing a fence for your property, make a careful determination of how and where your fence line will run.

It is important that the style of your fence echo the architecture of your house.

Picket fences are among the most common and pleasing types of fences in America.

The spacing between pickets permits a flow of sunlight that makes it possible to grow plants on either side.

The main drawback is the regular upkeep that picket fences require. To reduce the labor associated with frequent painting, consider staining the fence instead of painting it.

If you do use paint, start with an oil-based primer and then apply two layers of latex semigloss; periodic powerwashing will keep the fence clean. Or, use one of the new vinyl fences currently available. Made of PVC, they look very much like wood, and never rot or need painting.

Local contractors offer a wide assortment of good fencing. But before you buy, be sure to get a number of estimates—prices have a tendency to vary widely.

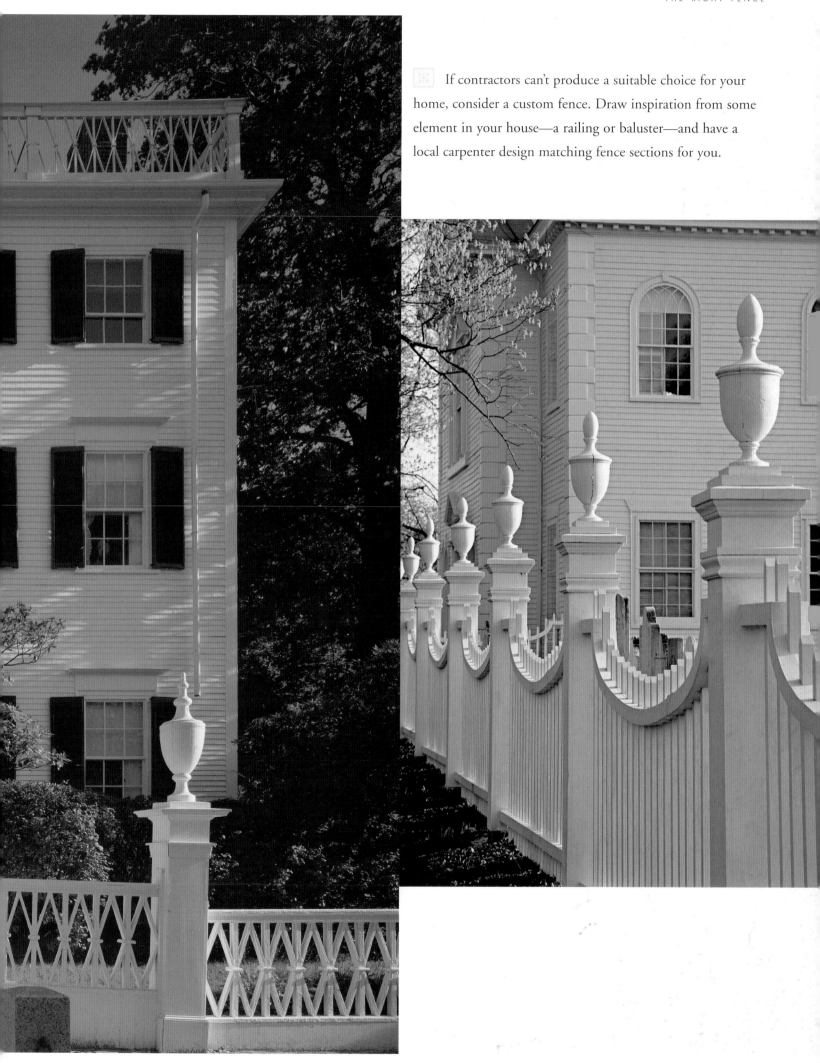

If contractors can't produce a suitable choice for your home, consider a custom fence. Draw inspiration from some element in your house—a railing or baluster—and have a local carpenter design matching fence sections for you.

Deck
Design

◈ Decks create transitions between the house and the yard.

◈ When considering whether to build a deck, think about whether you really want one at all or whether a terrace would better suit your needs.

◈ Terraces have a number of benefits over decks: Constructing one generally doesn't require licensed plans and a building permit, as a deck does; they can be easier to design, and generally yield a more aesthetically pleasing result, especially if you take care to match the surfacing material to elements already in the house and around the yard.

Decks are a good choice when the yard's topography is such that a level surface is not easily achievable by other means— on top of a rocky outcrop, for instance.

Decks should be kept as low to the ground as possible; the final level should be no more than two or three feet above the existing grade.

In new houses, design the floor plan so that you have direct access from the kitchen or back levels more or less at ground level.

In existing homes, consider constructing a proper porch or balcony consistent with the architecture of the house.

The most commonly used material for deck construction has until very recently been pressure-treated wood, which is generally made from chemically treated pine. The disadvantage of this material is that it can't generally be painted or stained for months after installation, and can often splinter, which is an important consideration if babies or children will be crawling on it. Given its dubious environmental legacy, it is falling out of favor.

Pressure-treated wood presents a waste disposal issue: leftover bits and pieces cannot be burned (the smoke is toxic), and many landfills and transfer stations have labeled the material environmentally hazardous and are refusing to accept it. Be sure your contractor settles all disposal issues before construction begins.

Two other wood choices are redwood and teak. Both are extremely durable and naturally resistant to rot, but expensive. Fir is a hard wood and less prone to splintering, but it must be rigorously maintained with preservatives every year or so. Plastic decking, made of new and recycled materials, is rapidly gaining in popularity. Extremely durable and available in a wide variety of colors, plastic decking looks and cuts very much like wood, with the tremendous benefit of never needing maintenance.

Edible Flowers: Facts and Tips

Do your research before you harvest. Some flowers, including sweet peas, iris, foxglove, amaryllis, lantana, lupines, clematis, datura, and others are poisonous. Others are simply unpalatable. To find out more, consult a reliable guide or website—www.campbellsnry.com/Handouts/edible plants.htm for a listing of edible flowers, their colors, and their flavors.

Include edible flowers in your landscape. Many varieties—including calendula, nasturtiums, and marigolds—make excellent additions to both flower and vegetable gardens and can also be grown easily in containers.

Don't spray edible flowers with any form of pesticide: Remember—they are destined for your plate, not the vase.

Wash blossoms thoroughly and carefully before eating—first in salt water, then in clear, cold water—to remove all dirt and grit, as well as any tiny insect stowaways.

Flower petals can be added to most any recipe imaginable. Use roses, nasturtiums, and chive blossoms to make flavored butters; add roses to vinegar.

Flowers can also be pickled, candied, and condensed into syrups and liqueurs and can top cakes, tarts, hors d'oeuvres, and soups. Sprinkle petals over roasts or grilled fish, add them into sauces, and float them in pot of tea. For parties, color coordinate them with the décor or freeze them in ice cubes.

Six Tips for Top Tomato Flavor

Plant tomatoes in your sunniest spot—they need at least eight hours of sunlight a day to develop the fullest flavor.

Improve yields and flavor with mulch.

Fertilize with compost or rotted manure before planting. Go easy on the nitrogen or you'll wind up with fewer fruits with weaker flavor.

Apply flavor-producing trace minerals. Use rock dust or a kelp foliar spray.

Cage vines so fruit and foliage stay off the ground and in the air, where light and circulation are better.

Water consistently so soil moisture stays even. Too much water dilutes the taste; too little inhibits flavor production.

Start Your Own Rhubarb Patch

Rhubarb is best started from rooted crowns, whether it is a division passed along from generation to generation or between friends, by those thinning out their patch or a potted plant from a nursery.

Acquiring local nursery stock ensures that the crown will be suited to your garden's conditions when starting your own patch in the early spring.

Each division should be about the size of your fist and have at least one healthy bud.

The best conditions for growing rhubarb is in full sun or partial shade in well-drained, fertile soil that is rich in organic matter.

Start your patch by putting about four inches of aged manure in the bottom of a deep (12 to 18 inches, depending on the size of your crown) trench or hole—it is a hungry plant!

Cover with a few inches of loamy soil or compost, spacing each crown approximately three to four feet apart. Then cover with additional soil and compost mix; the growing bud should now be one to two inches below the soil surface.

Spread a two- to four-inch layer of mulch over your newly planted patch and water the plants well. The mulch will help fend off weeds as well as keep the soil moist and the crowns from drying out.

Begin harvesting the stalks in the spring. Look for the thick stalks and gently twist and snap the stems near the crown with your hand. Harvest just a couple of stalks from your plants the first year.

As each spring and fall come around, rejuvenate your patch with a thick layer of nutrient-rich compost or manure. A well-tended, harvested patch can produce for up to 20 years.

When the middle stalks get spindly and small, it's time to divide. In the spring, when the first new sprouts appear, dig up and separate the crowns.

Party in the Garden

✻ Take advantage of the hard work you put into caring for your garden all summer long. Plan a late-summer harvest party.

✻ Plan the party around the juicy tomatoes, crisp cucumbers and all the just-gathered blooms in your own backyard.

✻ Ask your friends to bring berries, peppers, tomatoes, and flowers from their own gardens.

Garden-inspired party favors can use up end-of-summer vegetables. Snip favorites such as hydrangea blossoms and baby cabbages that have just begun to change color. Place them in clay pots for your friends to take home.

Use your garden pails and buckets to add sprays of color throughout your backyard. Use them to hold flowers for a centerpiece or line them up to create a path leading to your party site.

It is helpful to plan your next year's garden while looking at your present one. Ask your guests to share their garden experiences. Perhaps this exchange can provide new and adventurous ideas for future gardens.

Hydrangeas— Dramatic Seasonal Arrangements

After most flowering shrubs and perennials have gone for the season, hydrangeas stage a brilliant transformation from the sky blues, purples, and pinks into beautiful autumnal hues. Here are some tips for capturing their beauty and drama:

Harvest hydrangeas in the morning, after the dew has evaporated and before the midday heat threatens to wilt the flowers.

Look for blemish-free blooms. Those with complex hues indicate that they have just matured past their summer peak.

Cut the stems as long as possible, and remove the leaves.

For a show-stopping bouquet, bundle several stems together with a velvet ribbon and place the arrangement in a vase with a few inches of water.

If you don't replace the water in the vase after the flowers have absorbed it, the bouquet will dry in place and the arrangement will retain its shape and vibrancy.

Or fill a galvanized pail with a bunch of hydrangeas.

Create a flower ball by tying a ribbon around a sphere of florists's oasis, make holes with a knitting needle, chopstick, or skewer, then push in individual hydrangea florets interspersed with stephanotis.

To form a wreath, tie together bunches of flowers with raffia, and then attach them to a wire wreath base.

Make a garland by stringing bunches of hydrangea together with raffia.

Gravel Walks
& Drives

The marvelous crunch, crunch, crunch of gravel under-foot suggests that, for a brief moment, you may have left behind the thudding tarmac of modern age, and entered a slower-paced, more elegant world. A gravel walk lends a country air to the landscape and evokes country lanes and garden paths.

The amount of maintenance that a new gravel drive or walkway may require is greatly exaggerated.

Gravel needs to be raked once a year and occasionally weeded in low-traffic areas.

The installation of an average gravel drive is generally half as expensive as hard paving.

When it comes to snowplowing, it is important to remember that ground and gravel are very often already frozen before snow builds up. Therefore, the surface is rock-hard and can be plowed or shoveled just like any hard paving.

If an early snow falls, then just remember to raise the blade of the plow or snow blower slightly off the surface.

Gravel paths are problematic on sites that slope more than 20 degrees, as tire and foot traffic, as well as gravity will carry the gravel downhill.

Gravel needs to be contained by edging. This holds the secret to keeping gravel walks and drives easy to care for. Large cobblestones, sometimes called Belgian blocks, look pleasing and keep the gravel from leaking into adjoining areas.

Steel, tiles, bricks, or river rocks are other possibilities for edging material.

Gravel comes in a wide range of colors. The color palette available to you will depend on where you live, as gravel is generally mined locally. Given its extreme weight, the price of gravel will be lower if it has not incurred the high cost of shipping from faraway locations.

Pay attention to the type of stone offered. While crushed stone binds well and is required for under-layment, the jagged edges are visually hard on the eyes as well as the feet.

Quarter-inch river-washed peastone has been tumbled naturally in riverbeds and makes a smooth and pleasing top surface.

To build a proper gravel walk or drive, the base should be excavated to at least a foot deep and then compacted.

The excavation is filled successively with rough debris on the bottom to a depth of two or three inches, then with one-inch crushed stone up to two or three inches of the top, and then completely compacted.

Two or three inches of river-washed gravel should be placed on the top, com-pacted, and raked level.

287

Borderlines

※ Edgings can be important design elements in your garden.

※ Borderlines can create eye-catching patterns, define the perimeters of beds and paths, and produce an overall effect of tidiness.

※ An edging dividing a flower bed from the lawn can protect overflowing plants by keeping the mower at a distance.

The edging eliminates the need for hand-trimming the grass adjacent to the bed.

The choice of material used for the edging is a personal one.

Some possibilities include: flagstones, bricks (over-lapped on an angle, or placed end to end), railroad ties, and terra-cotta curbing tiles.

The edging material can be set in a bed of sand for stability.

Garden centers sell commercially made metal and plastic strips that can be used to keep stones or bricks in place. These work particularly well for following contours.

Whichever materials you do choose, it is good to keep in mind how they will look with your plantings.

A Grass Roots Project—Tips for Grass in and Around Your Garden

Beautiful lawns don't just appear; there is much work to be done in order to get a lush expanse of green grass on your property.

First you must assess the property's moisture level and take note of how much sun or shade it receives.

Then you are ready to choose the appropriate type of grass for your lawn.

Lawn grass comes in two types—cool-season and warm-season.

Cool-season grasses are good for Northern climates. It stays green in the winter but may turn brown in very hot and dry weather.

Cool-season grasses are generally planted in mixtures, including Kentucky bluegrass, fine fescues, perennial rye grass, and bent grass. They can be put in either as seed or as sod, and are best mowed high.

Warm-season grasses are good for Southern climates, but not recommended for Northern ones as they stay green in hot weather but go dormant in the winter.

Warm-season grasses are: Bermuda, St. Augustine, zoysia, and carpet. These are generally used individually, started as plugs or sod, and are best mowed close.

Healthy grass needs proper care and fertilizing. A high-nitrogen fertilizer should be applied twice a year, in spring and fall.

If you need to use weed-killer, opt for a low-toxic type with short-term residual impact such as glyphosfate.

Never mow a wet lawn. It is difficult to cut because the grass lies flat, and also will result in a ragged cut.

Making a Country Garden in the City

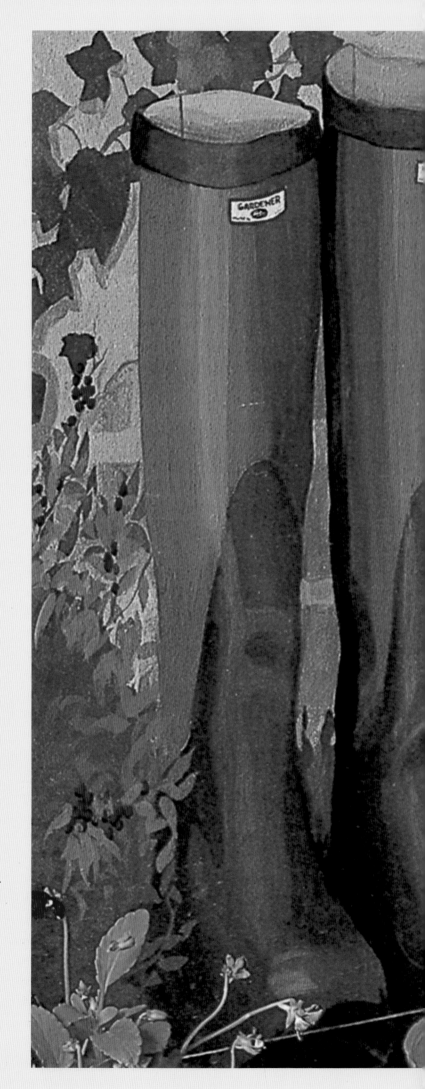

Limited space will be one of the hurdles to overcome when planting a garden in the city.

Try restricting flowers to a single border running along the walls or partitions of your space. That way you have fashioned an inner area upon which you can plant grass or lay brick or stone for a sitting area.

Don't let a single border of flowers cramp your style—go for a dramatic look in the style of an English cottage garden.

A romantic, untamed look can be achieved by mixing perennials, annuals, herbs, and roses.

Pay special attention to fragrance and interacting shapes and stagger the plants in height.

Successful gardens must evolve in stages. After one year you may have a full border, but then more autumn plantings may be required to extend the blooming season into August and September.

Limited storage space may also be a problem for city gardens. You will probably accrue a vast collection of pots, tools, and other garden paraphernalia.

If you have the room, try a simple and inexpensive storage shed made out of plywood. Paint the shed a neutral color so that it blends right in. Try a special painting technique to add texture or a weatherworn look.

One way to "fool the eye" is with a type of decorative painting called trompe l'oeil—when a flat rendering creates the illusion of three dimensions.

Popular trompe l'oeil techniques include sponging or ragging on color to create the look of stone or stucco, or detailed pictorial work for the illusion of an ivy-covered shed.

When working outdoors it is important to use weather-resistant, colorfast primer, paints and stains.

301

Country Abundance— Low- Maintenance Annuals

The best way to produce a season's worth of blooms with little trouble is to choose annuals that germinate quickly from seeds.

An easy annual garden is best cultivated with plants that require minimum watering, are pest resistant, and grow thickly enough to suppress weeds and create masses of color.

Many annuals will perform well until the first hard frost.

Use fish emulsion, a natural organic fertilizer, as it will help transplants adapt and will provide a boost for annuals planted in containers.

A light mulch will keep weeds at bay from seedlings.

Young plants benefit from thinning, which prevents overcrowding and reduces competition for light, water, and air.

Deep watering is usually more effective and time-efficient than superficial, frequent sprinklings.

Cosmos are easy-to-grow annuals that thrive in dry soil under warm weather conditions.

Their feathery foliage and varying heights make cosmos ideal backdrop plants in borders and good fillers.

Morning glories are vines that will grow rapidly up a post or arbor and will make an effective screen.

Marigolds have bright, pungent blooms that grow easily from seeds and will have an extended blooming period if they are sheared mid-season.

Climbing Vines

 Vines are a welcome addition to a country porch or arbor.

Climbing vines bring texture and color to small areas. They create shade and promote a general feeling of coolness.

Vines may be perennial, deciduous or evergreen, herbaceous or woody, sun- or shade-loving.

Different vines have different climbing methods and need to be matched to their supports with care. Some send out clinging tendrils and others hold on with twining stems or winding leafstalks called petioles. Some grip with small sticky adhesive discs.

Ivies, climbing hydrangeas, and creepers are effective for covering rough bricks or stone pillars and walls. Their rootlets or discs, are apt to cause wooden shingles and siding to heave and can damage wooden trellises.

Ivies are a poor choice for crumbling masonry because the greenery can force its way into the joints and weaken them.

Clematis, five-leaf akebias, and silver fleece are twining vines. These grow best on open or lattice supports, although some, like wisteria and Hall's honeysuckle, may overwhelm their supports if they are allowed.

Potting Tips

A great variety of plants grow well in containers. In addition to annuals and herbaceous perennials there are bulbs, corms and tubers, and small trees and shrubs.

Climbing vines, fruit, vegetables, miniature alpines and water-loving varieties can also be potted.

The key to success is choosing the right container.

Plants grow well in pots large enough to accommodate root development, yet small enough to show off the plant in proper scale.

Choose a pot that is an inch wider in diameter than the root ball.

In order to prevent the root from drowning, use a container with at least one hole in the bottom. If there are no holes place a layer of gravel or marble chips about one inch deep in the bottom of the container.

Standard recipe for soil preparation: one part perlite or coarse builder's sand, one part peat moss or compost, two parts good sterile potting soil.

The standard soil recipe should be adjusted accordingly for acid-loving plants such as hydrangeas and azaleas and for plants that prefer more alkaline conditions, such as clematis.

Check often to see whether the soil in the containers is dry, as nearly all potted annuals, perennials, trees, and shrubs require more frequent watering than plants growing right in the ground.

It is a good idea to feed liquid fertilizer once a week to annuals; potted perennials and roses can be fed about once every three weeks.

An initial high-nitrogen fertilizer feeding will promote fast growth of fruiting plants and perennials. A high-potassium liquid tomato fertilizer that encourages heavy flowering should follow this.

Clever Containers

A wide range of commercially made containers are available to gardeners, but outdoor planters can be created from almost any object that will hold soil and is water resistant.

Creative country-style examples include an old enamel roasting pan filled with posies, a hollow log overflowing with geraniums, or a galvanized tin bucket with marigolds poking out of the top.

For large groupings of plants, wagons, wheelbarrows, and carts can be great cargoes for plants, as well as leaky rowboats and decommissioned canoes.

Traditional choices are terracotta pots, which are available in the usual round sizes and as oblong planters.

Other country-style containers are urns, barrels, wooden cases, and buckets.

Troughs and shallow bowls are appropriate for miniature rock gardens.

Freestanding tubs are perfect for water gardens and for portable herb gardens.

Planters can reflect a gardener's regional character or environment. New England gardeners may use retired lobster pots, clamming baskets, and cranberry scoops. California vineyard country gardens may make use of wine kegs as planters.

Temperature fluctuations, severe weather, and wind will affect potted plants more quickly than those growing in the ground. So take care to provide those containers with shelter as needed.

During the wintertime, plants left outdoors in a harsh climate—where the temperature dips below zero for a week at a time—need a burlap wrapper. Otherwise, a mulch of straw will protect the plant. Ceramic and terracotta containers should be stored in a shed or basement, away from the freeze and thaw cycle that will cause them to crack.

Whatever type of container you use should be thoroughly cleaned first because any existing algae, bacteria, or fertilizer deposits may still be present. A soap-and-water bath followed by a gentle rinse with diluted bleach (no more than one part bleach to nine parts water) will do the trick.

Using clever containers lets you fill the nooks, crannies, doorways, and staircases around the house and yard with many types of blooms.

Container gardening has other benefits: apartment dwellers and those with small gardens can use pots of flowers to add interest to doorsteps or room corners.

Containers also permit gardeners to create microclimates best suited to individual species, and to nurture plants in customized conditions.

Crafts

Making Dried Flowers and Potpourri

Techniques for drying flowers have changed little since Victorian times. Flowers are dried by letting them hang upside down in bunches in a dry, dark, well-ventilated room or by layering them in silica gel or borax. Nowadays, herbs can be dried in the microwave.

Choosing Flowers

On a warm, sunny day, pick the most perfect-looking blooms at the peak of their maturity. Be sure that any morning dew or rain has evaporated.

If there is still moisture in the flower heads: allow the stemmed flowers to stand in 2 to 3 inches of warm water until the heads are completely dry.

Pick more than twice as many flowers as you think you will need since flowers may shrink, fade, or fall apart with any drying method.

Drying times will vary from days to weeks, depending on the flower and the drying environment.

With all types of drying methods, wait until the leaves and petals are as dry as paper and the stems snap apart when they are bent.

Hang Drying

The hang-drying method works well for flowers with small heads and twiggy stalks such as statice, baby's breath, everlasting, lavender, clover, bachelor's buttons, Chinese lanterns, hydrangeas, and most herbs.

Attics are often the best drying spaces.

You can experiment with different drying places by hanging flowers of the same type in different spots at the same time and then comparing color retention and drying times.

Strip the first few inches of leaves off the stems. With cotton string, tie the flowers together in small bunches and leave the string ends long. Fasten the loose ends to a peg, rafter, nail, clothesline, or other support so that air can circulate around the flowers.

Silica Gel or Borax Method

The shapes and colors of large flowers with delicate petals will be best preserved using this method. The scents, however, will not last.

Use on roses, chrysanthemums, daisies, carnations, pansies, and marigolds.

Crushed silica gel is available from craft and floral supply shops. Always follow the directions accompanying these items.

Begin by pouring a 2 inch layer of silica gel or borax in a large plastic box. Strip or cut the leaves, and cut off the stem about 2 to 3 inches from the flower head. (If you like, dry the leaves and stems separately).

Let some grains lay in between the petals so that each can be supported by the substance and can retain its shape.

Place each flower face down in the gel or borax, being careful that the flowers do not touch.

Completely cover the flowers by pouring more grain around and over them.

Place a test flower in each box, using a little marker to help you locate the bloom. Check the test flower until its texture is like taffeta—that is how you will know the flowers are finished drying.

To remove the flowers, place a spatula under the flower head and work it out carefully. Using a watercolor brush, remove any grains that cling to the dried flower petals.

Potpourri

Use 4 cups of partially dried petals such as chamomile, roses, honeysuckle, lilac, violets, lily of the valley, nasturtium, carnations, and white jasmine. The partially dried flowers best absorb and retain scented oils.

Add 1 tablespoon of herbs or spices such as cloves, allspice, cinnamon, lemon balm, etc.

Add 1/3 cup of powdered fixative, such as orrisroot, and 3 drops of essential oil—both are available at floral supply and craft shops. Add citrus peel or a bit of cologne or brandy. (These ingredients can also be used to revitalize an old, weak potpourri).

Mix all the items together and place in airtight jars. Let stand for 4 weeks, stirring once or twice each week.

To best retain the scent, keep potpourri in a covered container and open only when you want to release the scent.

Quick Drying

This method works well for scented leaves such as geraniums (which are available in orange, lemon, peppermint, and vanilla fragrances), mint, sage, bay laurel, rosemary, and thyme.

Spread the leaves on a rack or baking sheet covered in cheesecloth and place in a 90° oven. Leave the door open, and occasionally stir the leaves. Smaller, drier leaves take about 1 minute; thicker leaves take up to 3 minutes.

Flat Drying

The flat drying method is recommended for drying potpourri ingredients such as lemon and orange peel, eucalyptus, fragrant grasses, myrtle, basil, bay, lemon balm, rosemary, rose geranium, tarragon, and thyme.

Flat drying is also good for full-blown flowers such as roses, peonies, and dahlias, but they will not retain their shape and color.

333

Place the flowers on window screening supported by blocks so that air can circulate all around them.

You can also use a coarse mesh, such as hardware cloth, slipping the stems through the mesh so that the flower heads don't get flattened on one side.

Turn the flowers every other day.

Finishing for Arrangements

To protect dried flowers for arranging, temporarily stick their stems in a piece of plastic foam so that they will be upright.

In a well-ventilated area, spray the flowers with a few light coats of clear acrylic and let them dry.

Make a Berry Wreath

Welcome late-summer guests to your door with a colorful berry-dressed wreath. Using fresh-cut vines gathered from the garden, you can make this festive decoration in less than an hour.

MATERIALS:

A 10" to 12" heavy-gauge wire ring
pruning shears
gloves (to protect hands from thorny vines)
a spool of lightweight wire (green can be used to blend with the foliage)
fresh berries on their vines

Place wire ring on work surface.

Wrap short lengths of berry vines around ring, always working with thick to thin vines running in the same direction on ring and tucking under the ends.

Wind wire around vines and twist to secure the ring; trim off extra wire.

Attach a 10" piece of wire to top of completed wreath and form a loop to suspend.

TIPS: To make a fuller wreath, intertwine two or three layers of vines. To attach blueberries, wire the berries and parts of their bushes onto the vines. Fresh berry wreaths last a whole day.

Vintage Fabrics

Vintage fabrics are wonderful collectibles. They have bold colors, imaginative patterns, and a softness that comes with decades of use and cleaning.

When buying vintage fabrics, look for pieces in good condition with minimal staining. Cotton fabrics are especially easy to work with on a sewing machine, and most can be machine washed.

Before shopping online for these fabrics, familiarize yourself with current prices by attending flea markets and antique shows. Web sites such as Amazon.com Auctions (auctions.amazon.com) and eBay (ebay.com) are good sources for this material.

Fabric Projects to Try

Craft projects are a wonderful way to make use of fabric remnants—scraps of tablecloths, single napkins, unfinished quilt blocks—as well as vintage buttons and dressmaker's trimmings.

Colorful covers for sofa or bed pillows

Curtains for a kitchen or kid's room

Decorative doilies or table runners

Pieced or appliquéd quilts

Fabric-wrapped photo frames

Carriers for eyeglasses or checkbooks

Simple drawstring bags for gifts

Passport-size travel purses

Handmade cloth dolls

Matching pot holders or oven mitts.

Pressed-Leaf Curtains

Welcome fall into your home by decorating with the season's natural resources.

Collect leaves of varying hues with long stems intact.

Dry leaves thoroughly: Press between two sheets of waxed paper with a medium-hot iron for 10 seconds. Allow to cool.

Peel away paper.

Hang by attaching the stems to the top of sheer linen curtains with café clips.

Decorating with Buttons

Collect buttons of all sizes.

Flea markets are good places to find tons of buttons. Look for themes and sort by color or material type—such as pearlized or wooden buttons.

Decide on your design first. Then organize your buttons accordingly on your work surface.

Find ordinary picture frames or wooden or tin boxes with lids.

Place frame or box on a flat surface. If your design involves different sized buttons, attach large buttons with hot glue first, then begin filling in the gaps with smaller buttons.

You can even add faux pearls or small metallic pieces of glass for a shimmering effect.

Romantic Crafts

✷ Pretty ribbons wrapped around rose stems protect fingers from prickly thorns.

✷ Make a graceful heart-shaped wreath. Bend a wire clothes hanger into a heart shape and weave jasmine or grapevine around the form. Use florist wire to attach dried rosebuds and tie with ribbon.

✷ Using craft glue, affix found objects — small stones or sea glass to a love letter or favorite poem.

Create a heart-shaped silk pincushion stuffed with polyester batting.

Satisfy your sweetheart's sweet tooth with homemade cupcakes sprinkled with colored sugar and dressed in festive red-and-white paper baking cups.

A vellum envelope can conceal two heart-shaped shortbread cookies. To attach a bow, punch a hole in the corner and slip a red ribbon through it.

Personalize crisp white wrapping paper with punches of pink. Satin ribbon secures a bunch of roses and a vintage beaded flower to the gift box. Rickrack frames a heartfelt sentiment and a heart-shaped button handstitched to stock note-card paper.

Ornament a ticking pillowcase with felt hearts cut out with pinking shears.

Enhance a velvet heart with a button collection, or create a heart collage from assorted wallpaper or fabric swatches.

Paint Your Headboard a Dreamy Shade

Repainting your headboard can give your room just the lift it needs!

If existing paint is in poor condition, use paint remover and follow manufacturer's instructions, then use mineral spirits to remove any residue.

If the paint is in good condition, just wash the surface with an all-purpose cleaner and allow to dry completely.

Use sandpaper and steel wool to sand the surface.

Fill any deep holes with caulk or wood filler, sand those areas, vacuum, and then prime. Your headboard is now ready for painting.

For best results, use a quality brush.

To apply the paint, dip the brush into the can, so about one-quarter of the bristles are covered. Press the brush against the inside of the can's rim to remove excess paint.

Stroke the brush back and forth over the surface. Brush away any drips that form as quickly as possible.

Handcrafted
Journals

Personalize a keepsake, poem, or note for yourself or a friend to treasure . . .

Using textured paper, secure a scrolled poem or quotation with length of ribbon, string, or raffia. Thread the ends of the tie through a miniature trinket such as a button or seashell.

Use foliage or pressed flowers from your garden to create decorative edges on a photograph, postcard, memorable ticket stub or a map.

Embellish your own journal with items that can be found around the house or at your local stationary store: Rubber stamps, colored inks, art papers, or swatches of fabric snipped from an old favorite piece of clothing.

Make a concertina-style journal: weave strips of ribbon through evenly punched holes into both sides of thick paper cards. Attach keepsake items with dressmaker's pins, or glue and pen your own captions, or use alphabet rubber stamps to identify the memorabilia.

Buy a journal and personalize it for a gift: Cover the front and back of a blank book with plain linen fabric; hand stitch initials onto a smaller piece of fabric and sew or glue the embroidered piece to the front cover of the book.

How to Frame a Picture

Create a custom-look frame for your family photographs by choosing museum-quality materials, including mat board and photo corners.

Ready-to-use mats and frames can often be found for standard-size photographs, while images or frames of irregular sizes or shapes will need custom-cut mats, which can be ordered at frame shops (bring the photo with you for best fit).

Cut-to-size glass and Plexiglas with UV protection is easily obtained at industrial glass suppliers.

Gather your materials—a bottom mat, top mat with cut window, glass, frame, and photo corners—on a clean surface in a well-lit area.

Align the photograph on the bottom mat and attach with photo corners.

Place the window mat over the photograph.

Pick up the bottom mat, photograph, and top mat and carefully turn all three over. Set top mat against glass in frame. Seal the frame; hang or display the finished piece away from direct sunlight.

Making Children's Memento Boxes

Children are born collectors. Why not help them file their treasures in an orderly way? A few shoe boxes, a bit of fabric, adhesive-backed wrapping paper, some glue, and some labels are all you need.

Center a shoe box on the covering of your choice and fold the fabric or paper so that it reaches up the sides and overlaps about one inch inside the box. Carefully miter the corners and trim off any excess.

Now spread white household glue on the outside of the box, place the box on the trimmed fabric or paper, and smooth the covering up the sides and ends of the box and along the interior perimeter. Do the same with the lid.

Decorate with ribbon or braid or buttons or lace, as you wish.

Let your child think of a good name for the collection and ask him or her to print the title on a label that can be glued to the end of the box.

Tailor Your Headboard for a Personal Touch

Just pad a piece of plywood with foam.

Cover with the upholstery-grade fabric of your choice.

Bolt the finished headboard to an ordinary metal bed frame.

It's as easy as putting a (padded plywood) letter into a (fabric) envelope. Sewing is minimal, and spray adhesive and fusible iron-on tape make gluing and hemming a snap.

MATERIALS:

3/4-inch plywood, 48 inches high and 54 inches wide (full or queen size; adjust width for twin or king size)

Metal bed frame

Drill with 5/16-inch drill bit

Two pieces of 1- or 2-inch-thick urethane foam: each 55 inches wide and 49 inches high (or 1 inch larger than the plywood)

Duct tape

3M "77" spray adhesive

Four 1/4-inch carriage bolts

Sturdy fabric: two pieces, each 56 inches wide and 51 inches high (or 1 inch wider and 2 inches longer than the padded plywood)

Step 1:

Stand plywood at head of bed. Use holes in bed frame as a guide to mark and drill holes in plywood, two on each side, one atop the other, where carriage bolts will eventually go.

Step 2:

Apply spray adhesive to front and back of plywood; apply a piece of foam to each side. Leave a 1-inch overlap of foam at top and sides. Apply spray adhesive to top and side edges of foam. Let dry; pinch together to create a seam. Reinforce the joined seam with 1 1/2-inch duct tape. Note: Foam comes in

rolls 54 inches wide; we ran it sideways and glued the seams with spray adhesive, edge to edge.

Step 3:

Next, stitch fabric together on three sides, right sides facing, leaving 1 inch top and side seams; leave bottom edge open. Turn right side out.

Step 4:

Pull finished slipcover over padded headboard. Stand headboard in place. Tuck a 2-inch hem along bottom edge and pin in place. Locate bolt holes in plywood using a long needle; mark with chalk. Remove slipcover and sew around the four chalk marks with a zigzag stitch; cut out slits. Hem bottom edge of slipcover using iron-on tape. Pull finished slipcover over headboard, slide bolts through holes and secure.

Tips for a Terrific Tag Sale

Before scouring your attic and closets for goods decide when the sale should be held and where the best venue would be.

Contact your local town hall or department of commerce to find out about any necessary permits and parking regulations.

Place classified ads in the local newspaper and tell all your friends and acquaintances about your plans.

Very early on the morning of the sale, hang signs around your neighborhood. Use big block letters and keep directions simple.

Sort all objects by price range—"All items on this table $1.00" or "All items in this box 25¢." Or sort by category—toys, books, linens, glass. You can also categorize by destination in the home—"Garden," "Library," "Kitchen."

For those pieces that you think may have a significant value, consult a price guide to determine what to charge.

Clearly mark prices on each item.

Have plenty of change on hand.

If hosting a sale with friends, individual money jars for each vendor will help eliminate payment confusion.

When setting up your tables, keep in mind that pieces look better if you cluster them by color, size, or style. This approach may even encourage customers to buy multiple pieces so that they can achieve the same look at home.

Set out a table of baked goods, caramel apples, and lemonade or cider. This will add a nice, old-fashioned touch to the tag sale.

If there is no rain date set, then have some sort of tent or shelter ready to place delicate items under. Tables displaying books, textiles, and paper goods should not sit out in the rain.

Country
Recipes

Cooking
with
Rhubarb

Rhubarb-Almond Muffins

MAKES 16 MUFFINS

Vegetable-oil cooking spray

2/3 pound rhubarb, tops removed and ends trimmed

2 1/2 cups unsifted all-purpose four

3/4 cup chopped almonds

1 teaspoon baking powder

1 teaspoon baking soda

1/4 teaspoon nutmeg

1/2 teaspoon salt

1/4 teaspoon ground cinnamon

1 cup firmly packed light brown sugar

1 1/4 cups buttermilk

1/2 cup vegetable oil

1 large egg

1 tablespoon vanilla extract

1/2 cup chopped pitted prunes

Heat oven to 375°F. Lightly coat sixteen 2 1/2-inch muffin-pan cups with cooking spray. Wash rhubarb stalks; coarsely chop and set aside.

In a large bowl, combine flour, almonds, baking powder, baking soda, nutmeg, salt, and cinnamon.

In a medium bowl with mixer on medium speed, beat brown sugar, buttermilk, oil, egg, and vanilla until combined. Stir into flour mixture just until moistened; the batter will be lumpy. Fold rhubarb and prunes into batter. Spoon batter into muffin cups.

Bake muffins until cake tester inserted in center of a muffin comes out clean, 18 to 20 minutes. Let cool in pans 5 minutes. Transfer muffins to a wire rack and let cool completely. Store in an airtight container for up to 3 days.

NUTRITION INFORMATION: per muffin—protein: 5 g; fat: 11 g; carbohydrate: 36 g; fiber: 2 g; sodium: 171 mg; cholesterol: 14 mg; calories: 252.

Rhubarb-Pecan Oatmeal Bars

MAKES 16 BARS

Vegetable oil cooking spray

1¹/2 cups unsifted all-purpose flour

1¹/2 cups old-fashioned rolled oats

1 cup firmly packed light brown sugar

1/2 teaspoon ground cinnamon

1/2 teaspoon salt

3/4 cup (1 ¹/2 sticks) butter, softened

2 cups thickened Chunky Rhubarb Sauce (recipe follows)

1/2 cup chopped pecans

Heat oven to 375°F. Lightly coat a 13- by 9-inch baking pan with cooking spray.

In a medium bowl, combine flour, oats, brown sugar, cinnamon, and salt. Add butter and stir with fork until mixture resembles coarse crumbs.

Press two-thirds of crumb mixture into bottom of pan. Spread thickened sauce evenly over crumb layer. Top with remaining crumb mixture and pecans.

Bake until top is golden and rhubarb sauce bubbles, 25 to 30 minutes. Let cool on wire rack to room temperature. Cut into 16 bars and store in airtight container for up to 3 days.

NUTRITION INFORMATION: per bar—protein: 3 g; fat: 12 g; carbohydrate: 35 g; fiber: 2 g; sodium: 164 mg; cholesterol: 23 mg; calories: 251.

Chunky Rhubarb Sauce

MAKES ABOUT 3¹/2 CUPS

2 pounds rhubarb, tops removed, ends trimmed, and
  cut into 1-inch pieces
3/4 cup sugar
1/3 cup fresh-squeezed orange juice
1 teaspoon grated orange rind
1/4 teaspoon ground nutmeg
1/4 teaspoon salt

In a 4-quart saucepan, combine rhubarb, sugar, orange juice, orange rind, nutmeg, and salt. Bring to a boil. Reduce heat to low, cover, and simmer until thickened, about 15 minutes. Cool to room temperature. Refrigerate until ready to use.

NUTRITION INFORMATION: per ¹/4 cup—protein: 6 g; fat: 0 g; carbohydrate: 14 g; fiber: 2 g; sodium: 41 mg; cholesterol: 0 mg; calories: 58.

Strawberry-Rhubarb Syrup

MAKES I ¹/4 CUPS

3/4 cup trimmed and chopped rhubarb
1/2 cup sliced strawberries
2/3 cup granulated sugar
1/2 cup water

In a 1-quart saucepan, combine rhubarb, strawberries, sugar, and water. Bring to a boil over medium-high heat; cook until rhubarb is very soft, about 15 minutes. Strain mixture into serving dish, discarding rhubarb-strawberry pulp. Store in an airtight container, refrigerated for up to 4 days.

NUTRITION INFORMATION: per 2-tablespoon serving—protein: 0.1 g; fat: 0g; carbohydrate: 14 g; fiber: 0.4 g; sodium: 1 mg; cholesterol: 0 mg; calories: 55.

Chutney-Glazed Pork Tenderloin

MAKES 4 SERVINGS

Vegetable-oil cooking spray
1 teaspoon hot paprika
1/2 teaspoon salt
1/4 teaspoon ground black pepper
1 boneless pork tenderloin (about 1 1/4 pounds)
1 cup Spicy Rhubarb Chutney (recipe follows)
Tortillas (optional)
Fresh cilantro sprigs (optional)

Heat oven to 350°F. Lightly coat bottom of roasting pan with cooking spray. In a small bowl, combine paprika, salt, and pepper. Sprinkle mixture over the pork.

Place pork in prepared roasting pan and roast 20 minutes. Brush 1/2 cup chutney over tenderloin and continue roasting until internal temperature reaches 160°F, 20 to 25 minutes longer, basting occasionally with pan drippings. Let rest 10 minutes before slicing.

Serve pork tenderloin with remaining chutney, tortillas, and cilantro, if desired.

NUTRITION INFORMATION: per serving without tortillas or cilantro—protein: 35 g; fat: 12 g; carbohydrate: 32 g; fiber: 4 g; sodium: 427 mg; cholesterol: 104 mg; calories: 351.

Spicy Rhubarb Chutney

MAKES 2 CUPS

1 1/4 pounds rhubarb, tops removed and ends trimmed
1/2 cup firmly packed light brown sugar
1/4 cup apple-cider vinegar
1/4 cup chopped onion
1/2 teaspoon ground coriander
1/2 teaspoon ground ginger
1/4 teaspoon dry mustard
1/4 teaspoon salt
1/3 cup chopped dried apricots
1/3 cup dried cherries
2 tablespoons chopped fresh cilantro leaves

Wash rhubarb stalks; coarsely chop and set aside.

In a 4-quart saucepan, combine brown sugar, vinegar, onion, coriander, ginger, mustard, and salt. Bring to a boil. Cook over high heat, uncovered, 3 minutes, stirring constantly. Stir in rhubarb, apricots, and cherries; reduce heat to medium-low and let simmer until rhubarb is just tender but not broken up, 10 to 15 minutes. Remove from heat, stir in cilantro, and let cool 10 minutes. Refrigerate until ready to use.

NUTRITION INFORMATION: per 1/4 cup—protein: 1 g; fat: 0.2 g; carbohydrate: 26 g; fiber: 3 g; sodium: 77 mg; cholesterol: 0 mg; calories: 104.

Country French Toast
MAKES 8 SLICES

3 large eggs

1 cup milk

2 teaspoons sugar

1 teaspoon vanilla extract

1/4 teaspoon salt

1 one-pound rectangular loaf unsliced challah or other
*   firm bread*

2 tablespoons vegetable oil

Strawberry-Rhubarb Syrup (recipe on page 367)

In a medium bowl, beat together eggs, milk, sugar, vanilla, and salt. Using a serrated knife, trim crust from bread; discard. Cut loaf crosswise into 8 equal slices.

Pour half of egg mixture into a 13- by 9-inch baking dish. Arrange bread slices in a single layer in dish; pour remaining egg mixture over bread slices. Set aside until bread absorbs all egg mixture—about 20 minutes. If desired, prepare bread to this point; cover and refrigerate several hours overnight.

When ready to serve, heat oven to 200°F. In large nonstick skillet, heat 2 teaspoons oil over medium-high heat. Add bread slices, several at a time, and cook until browned on both sides, adding remaining oil as needed. When slices are cooked through, transfer to a baking sheet and keep warm in preheated oven. Repeat with remaining slices. Serve with Strawberry-Rhubarb Syrup.

NUTRITION INFORMATION: per slice with 2 tablespoons syrup—protein: 8 g; fat: 9 g; carbohydrate: 45 g; fiber: 1 g; sodium: 399 mg; cholesterol: 82 mg; calories: 287.

Short Ribs with Asian-Rhubarb Sauce
MAKES 4 SERVINGS

SHORT-RIB MARINADE:

4 pounds beef short ribs

2 tablespoons vegetable oil

4 cloves garlic, finely chopped

2 tablespoons finely chopped fresh gingerroot

3/4 teaspoon salt

1/2 teaspoon ground black pepper

ASIAN-RHUBARB SAUCE:

1 can (14 1/2 ounces) reduced-sodium chicken broth

1/2 cup sake

2 tablespoons honey

1/2 pound rhubarb, tops removed and ends trimmed

1/4 cup prepared hoisin sauce

1/4 cup sugar

2 tablespoons apple-cider vinegar

1/4 teaspoon crushed red pepper

Prepare Short-Rib Marinade: Trim excess fat from short ribs. In a 6-quart Dutch oven, heat oil over medium heat. Add ribs and brown in batches, transferring browned ribs to a large bowl. Remove and discard all but 1 tablespoon of cooking liquid from Dutch oven. Return ribs to Dutch oven and add garlic, gingerroot, salt, and pepper. Cover and refrigerate 1 hour.

Prepare Asian-Rhubarb Sauce: Heat oven to 350°F. Add chicken broth, sake, and honey to marinade in Dutch oven. Place over medium-high heat and bring to a boil. Cover and transfer to oven; bake until ribs are tender, about 1 1/2 hours.

Wash and roughly chop rhubarb. In the bowl of a food processor fitted with metal blade, pulse until rhubarb is very finely chopped.

Transfer ribs to rack of a roasting pan. Pour cooking liquid and drippings from Dutch oven into a 4-cup measuring cup; skim off fat. Return 1/2 cup cooking liquid to Dutch oven and discard remaining liquid. Add rhubarb, hoisin sauce, sugar, vinegar, and red pepper. Bring to a boil. Cook 5 minutes more, stirring occasionally.

Brush some of the rhubarb mixture over ribs. Cook 15 minutes. Brush ribs with remaining rhubarb mixture and continue cooking until glazed, 15 to 20 minutes. Serve.

NUTRITION INFORMATION per serving—protein: 64 g; fat: 39 g; carbohydrate: 28 g; fiber: 2 g; sodium: 1,207 mg; cholesterol: 186 mg; calories: 741.

Make the Most of Your Garden-Fresh Rhubarb

Use rhubarb in your favorite recipes as soon as possible after it is harvested.

The leaves, which contain traces of oxalic acid, are actually poisonous; trim them right in the patch and turn them under the soil, where they replace spent nutrients.

In the kitchen, trim the ends and wash stalks thoroughly under cold running water and pat dry with a clean, dry towel.

Create recipe-ready amounts by cutting the stalks into 1-inch pieces and dividing them in to 4-cup batches.

Place each batch in a sealable plastic bag and store in the refrigerator for up to 3 days.

After 3 days the rhubarb begins to break down and becomes too moist to really work with.

You can freeze rhubarb for en extended period of time, but you will lose some of the fresh texture and flavor. Because the patch will continue to produce stalks through the early summer, it is best to harvest only the amount you need for a particular recipe.

Nantucket
Holiday

Lemon Clam Dip

MAKES 1 3/4 CUPS

2 cans (6¹/2-ounces each) minced clams, drained and
    juice reserved

2 tablespoons minced fresh chives

2 tablespoons lemon juice

1 clove garlic, minced

¹/4 teaspoon hot red-pepper sauce

¹/4 teaspoon ground black pepper

1 package (8 ounces) cream cheese, softened

3 tablespoons sour cream

Assorted breads (for serving)

Fresh chives, snipped into ¹/2-inch lengths (optional)

In a small bowl, combine clams, 3 tablespoons reserved clam juice (discard remaining clam juice or save for another use), chives, lemon juice, garlic, hot red-pepper sauce, and black pepper.

In a medium bowl, blend together cream cheese and sour cream. Add clam mixture and stir until well combined. Cover and refrigerate for at least 30 minutes before serving. Serve with assorted fresh breads and garnish with chives, if desired.

NUTRITION INFORMATION: per tablespoon with assorted breads—protein: 4 g; fat: 3 g; carbohydrate: 1 g; fiber: 0 g; sodium: 40 mg; cholesterol: 18 mg; calories: 52.

Wilted Spinach and Red Onion Salad

MAKES 6 ONE-CUP SERVINGS

2 tablespoons olive oil

¹/2 medium red onion, thinly sliced

3 cloves garlic, finely chopped

2 one-pound bags small spinach leaves

2 tablespoons water

³/4 tablespoon salt

2 tablespoons sherry vinegar

¹/2 teaspoon ground black pepper

In a large skillet, warm olive oil over medium heat. Add onion and garlic; cook 1 minute. Stir in spinach, water, and salt. Cook 1 minute or just until spinach leaves start to wilt. Remove from heat and transfer to large serving bowl. Sprinkle salad with vinegar and black pepper. Serve.

NUTRITION INFORMATION: per serving—protein: 5 g; fat: 5 g; carbohydrate: 7 g; fiber: 5 g; sodium: 386 mg; cholesterol: 0 mg; calories: 80.

Johnnycakes with Nantucket Bay Scallops and Horseradish Cream
MAKES ABOUT 2 DOZEN JOHNNYCAKES

1 cup yellow cornmeal

1 tablespoon all-purpose flour

1 teaspoon baking powder

1/2 teaspoon baking soda

1/2 teaspoon ground black pepper

1/2 teaspoon salt

1 cup (1/2 pound) bay scallops, quartered

3/4 cup fresh or frozen corn kernels

1 cup buttermilk

1 large egg

1 tablespoon maple syrup

1 tablespoon minced roasted red pepper

1/2 cup crème fraîche or sour cream

1 tablespoon prepared horseradish

1/8 teaspoon ground white pepper

1/3 cup vegetable oil, divided

Chopped fresh chives (optional)

In a large bowl, mix together cornmeal, flour, baking powder, baking soda, black pepper, and salt. Add scallops and corn.

In a medium bowl, whisk together buttermilk, egg, and maple syrup. Fold in red pepper. Pour buttermilk mixture into cornmeal mixture and stir until just combined. Set aside.

In a small bowl, whisk together the crème fraîche, horseradish, and white pepper. Cover and refrigerate until ready to serve.

Heat oven to 225°F. In a large nonstick skillet, heat 1 tablespoon of oil over medium-high heat. In heaping tablespoons, drop batter onto hot skillet and cook until edges of johnnycakes begin to brown, about 2 to 3 minutes. Turn johnnycakes over and continue cooking until cooked through, 2 to 3 minutes longer.

Transfer johnnycakes to a serving platter that can be kept warm in preheated oven. Repeat process to cook all johnnycakes. Serve with horseradish cream and chives, if desired.

NUTRITION INFORMATION: per johnnycake—protein: 3 g; fat: 5 g; carbohydrate: 7 g; fiber: 0.6 g; sodium: 108 mg; cholesterol: 14 mg; calories: 81.

Grilled Lobster with Lime-Bay Butter
MAKES 6 SERVINGS

3 fresh lobsters, 1 1/2 pounds each

1/2 cup (1 stick) butter

1/4 cup fresh lime juice

1/2 teaspoon crushed bay leaf

1/4 teaspoon ground black pepper

1/4 teaspoon salt

Lime wedges (optional)

Bay leaves (optional)

Bring 3 inches of water in an 8-quart saucepan to boiling over high heat. Add lobsters to the pan, cover, and cook 10 minutes. Remove lobsters from saucepan and let cool.

Heat grill to medium. In a 1-quart saucepan, heat butter, lime juice, crushed bay leaf, black pepper, and salt over low heat for 10 minutes.

When lobsters are cool to the touch, cut in half lengthwise and brush cut side with lime-bay butter. Place lobsters, cut-side down, on grill, about 4 inches from heat source. Cook 5

*Jenny Cakes with Nantucket Bay Scallops
and Horseradish Cream*

Lemon Clam Dip with Assorted Breads

Grilled Lobster with Lime Bay Butter

*Sirloin and Summer Vegetable Kebabs
with Fire Cracker Sauce*

Spicy Tomato Jam

Americana Potato Salad

Wilted Spinach and Red Onion Salad

*Fresh Berry Shortcake with Spiced Syrup
Cranberry Chunk Ice Cream*

minutes. Carefully turn lobsters over, brush with butter, and continue grilling until lobster meat is cooked through—about 5 minutes longer. Transfer lobsters to a serving plate and garnish with lime wedges and bay leaves, if desired. Serve one-half lobster per person.

NUTRITION INFORMATION: per serving—protein: 32 g; fat: 17 g; carbohydrate: 2 g; fiber: 0 g; sodium: 728 mg; cholesterol: 203 mg; calories: 291.

Sirloin and Summer Vegetable Kabobs with Firecracker Sauce

MAKES 12 KABOBS

FIRECRACKER SAUCE:

1/4 cup fresh lime juice

1/4 cup maple syrup

2 tablespoons ketchup

2 tablespoons olive oil

2 tablespoons soy sauce

4 cloves garlic, finely chopped

1 teaspoon crushed red-pepper flakes

1/2 teaspoon ground black pepper

1/2 teaspoon grated lime rind

1/2 teaspoon salt

KABOBS:

1 1/4 pounds boneless beef top loin or sirloin steak, cut into 1 1/4-inch cubes

3 medium onions, quartered

2 medium yellow squash, cut crosswise into 1-inch slices

2 medium zucchini, cut crosswise into 1-inch slices

1 large red bell pepper, seeded and cut into 1-inch pieces

12 wooden skewers (8-inch), soaked in water 15 minutes

Sprig of thyme (optional)

Small hot peppers (optional)

Prepare Firecracker Sauce: In medium bowl, whisk together lime juice, maple syrup, ketchup, olive oil, soy sauce, garlic, crushed red-pepper flakes, black pepper, lime rind, and salt. Makes about 1 cup. Set aside.

On 1 skewer, randomly arrange 2 pieces of cubed steak and one piece each of onion, yellow squash, zucchini, and red pepper. Repeat to make 11 more kabobs. Place kabobs in large baking dish.

Pour 3/4 cup of Firecracker Sauce over kabobs in baking dish. Reserve 1/4 cup for brushing the kabobs as they cook. Let kabobs stand for 15 minutes.

Heat grill to medium. Grill kabobs about 4 inches above heat source for 5 minutes, turning frequently. Brush kabobs with reserved Firecracker Sauce. Cook 5 to 7 minutes longer or until desired doneness is reached.

NUTRITION INFORMATION: per skewer—protein: 14 g; fat: 7 g; carbohydrate: 8 g; fiber: 0.6 g; sodium: 324 mg; cholesterol: 36 mg; calories: 147.

Americana Potato Salad

MAKES 8 CUPS

3 pounds small red potatoes, quartered

1 1/2 teaspoons salt

1/2 cup extra-virgin olive oil

1/4 cup tarragon or cider vinegar

1 teaspoon dried or 1 tablespoon fresh chopped tarragon leaves

1/2 teaspoon ground black pepper

1 cup chopped celery

1 cup finely chopped sweet onion

1/2 cup chopped green onions

2 tablespoons sweet pickle relish

4 large hard-boiled eggs, peeled and grated

1/2 cup mayonnaise

1/4 cup finely chopped roasted red pepper

4 strips crisp bacon, crumbled

In a large saucepan, combine potatoes, 1 teaspoon salt, and enough water to cover. Bring to a boil over high heat. Cook potatoes until fork-tender, 10 to 12 minutes. Drain potatoes and place in a large bowl.

In a small bowl, whisk together olive oil, vinegar, tarragon, remaining 1/2 teaspoon salt, and black pepper. Add olive-oil mixture to potatoes. Stir in celery, sweet and green onions, and pickle relish. Fold in eggs and mayonnaise. Cover and refrigerate for at least 2 hours or overnight.

Thirty minutes before serving, let potato mixture come to room temperature. Just before serving, fold in roasted red pepper and sprinkle with crumbled bacon.

NUTRITION INFORMATION: per 1/2 cup serving—protein: 4 g; fat: 14 g; carbohydrate: 24 g; fiber: 2 g; sodium: 241 mg; cholesterol: 57 mg; calories: 238.

Spicy Tomato Jam

MAKES 3 1/2 CUPS

1 cup cider vinegar

3/4 cup sugar

1/2 cup bourbon

3 pounds ripe plum tomatoes

1 teaspoon whole black peppercorns

8 whole allspice berries

8 whole cloves

1 teaspoon dried red-pepper flakes

1/2 teaspoon mustard seeds

1/2 teaspoon ground cumin

In a large bowl, combine vinegar, sugar, and bourbon. Stir to dissolve sugar. Set aside.

In a 5-quart nonreactive saucepan, bring 3 quarts of water to boil over high heat. Carefully drop tomatoes into boiling water and cook until skins of tomatoes start to split, 1 to 2 minutes. With slotted spoon, remove tomatoes and plunge into ice water. Let tomatoes cool to touch. Peel off tomato skins and discard. Coarsely chop tomatoes; set aside.

Meanwhile, in center of a small square of cheesecloth, combine peppercorns, allspice berries, cloves, red-pepper flakes, and mustard seeds. Tie cheesecloth up to make a spice bag using a piece of kitchen string.

In a 5-quart saucepan, combine tomatoes, vinegar mixture, the spice bag, and cumin. Bring mixture to a boil over high heat. Reduce heat to medium and cool 35 to 40 minutes, stirring occasionally, until liquid has evaporated. Remove from heat and let cool for 20 minutes.

Discard spice bag and divide tomato jam among gift jars or transfer to a container with a tight-fitting lid. Refrigerate until ready to use. The tomato jam will keep for 1 month, refrigerated.

NUTRITION INFORMATION: per 1/4-cup serving—protein: 1 g; fat: 0.2 g; carbohydrate: 16 g; fiber: 1 g; sodium: 8 mg; cholesterol: 0 mg; calories: 81.

Sparkling Cranberry Splash
MAKES 6 ONE-CUP SERVINGS

1 bottle vinho verde, chilled
1/3 cup cranberry-juice cocktail
Crushed ice
3 ripe white peaches, sliced (optional)
Mint sprigs (optional)

In a large pitcher, combine wine and cranberry-juice cocktail. Divide crushed ice and wine mixture among glasses. Garnish each glass with sliced peaches and a sprig of mint, if desired.

NUTRITION INFORMATION: per serving—protein: 0.5 g; fat: 0 g; carbohydrate: 8 g; fiber: 0.8 g; sodium: 7 mg; cholesterol: 0 mg; calories: 132.

Picnic Games

Lawn games such as badminton, horseshoes, and croquet are classic picnic games for kids and adults. They are ideal for picnics as they require a minimal amount of equipment and can be set up in minutes.

Soccer balls, softballs, mitts, footballs, and Frisbees are good for crowds as they are fun and don't require formal teams.

Hopscotch is a no mess, no fuss game—bring along big sticks of colorful chalk to create the course. The chalk washes away easily with a quick spray from a garden hose.

If you don't want to bring along any equipment, there are always 20 questions, hide-and-seek, charades, monkey-in-the-middle, duck-duck-goose, and relay races.

Cards, puzzles, and books work indoors as well as outside, and are just the right activities for winding down.

Fresh Berry Shortcake with Spiced Syrup

MAKES 6 SERVINGS

SPICED BERRIES:

1¹/2 cups water

1 cup granulated sugar

¹/3 fresh lemon juice

2 one-inch slices fresh gingerroot

1 three-inch cinnamon stick

1 star anise, crushed

1 vanilla bean, split

1 tablespoon cognac (optional)

1 pint (2 cups) fresh blueberries

1 pint (2 cups) fresh strawberries, hulled and halved

¹/2 pint (1 cup) fresh raspberries

SHORTCAKES:

2 cups self-rising all-purpose flour

3 tablespoons granulated sugar

¹/2 cup (1 stick) unsalted butter

3/4 cup milk

¹/2 cup plus 1 tablespoon heavy cream

1 teaspoon confectioners' sugar

Prepare Spiced Berries: In 2-quart saucepan, combine water, granulated sugar, lemon juice, gingerroot, cinnamon, star anise, and vanilla bean. Bring to boil over high heat. Reduce heat to medium and simmer for 25 minutes. Remove from heat and strain mixture through a fine sieve, discarding spices. Stir in cognac, if using, and set spice mixture aside to cool completely.

Add blueberries, strawberries, and raspberries to spice mixture. Set aside.

Prepare Shortcakes: Heat oven to 400°F. Lightly spray a baking sheet with vegetable-oil cooking spray. In a medium bowl, combine flour and granulated sugar. With pastry blender or 2 knives, cut in butter until mixture resembles

coarse crumbs. Stir in milk until very soft dough forms, being careful not to overwork the dough.

Divide the dough into six equal pieces and drop onto prepared baking sheet. Lightly pat each into a round and brush with 1 tablespoon heavy cream. Bake until shortcakes are golden brown—about 20 minutes. Transfer to wire rack and cool completely.

In a medium bowl, with mixer on high speed, beat remaining $1/2$ cup heavy cream and confectioners' sugar until stiff peaks form.

To assemble, cut each shortcake horizontally in half. Place each bottom half on a dessert plate. Spoon about $3/4$ cup of berry mixture over bottom half. Spoon a heaping tablespoon of whipped cream on top of berry mixture. Place matching shortcake half on top. Drizzle each plate with spiced syrup.

NUTRITION INFORMATION: per serving—protein: 7 g; fat: 26 g; carbohydrate: 88 g; fiber: 5 g; sodium: 480 mg; cholesterol: 76 mg; calories: 593.

Comfort
Foods

Corned-Beef Hash with Boston Brown Bread

MAKES 6 SERVINGS

1 pound (2¹/₂ cups) peeled and diced potatoes

1 pound unsliced cooked corned beef

3 tablespoons vegetable oil

1 cup chopped onion

2 cloves garlic, finely chopped

¹/₄ teaspoon salt

¹/₄ teaspoon ground black pepper

2 teaspoons coarse-grained prepared mustard

2 tablespoons butter

6 fried or poached eggs (optional)

Boston Brown Bread (recipe follows)

Place potatoes in a 2-quart saucepan and cover with water. Bring to a gentle boil over high heat; cool until fork-tender, about 10 minutes. Drain.

In a food processor with chopping blade, pulse corned beef until coarsely chopped, or shred by hand.

In a large cast-iron or non-stick skillet, heat oil over medium heat. Add onion and garlic; sauté until softened, about 5 minutes. Add potatoes, salt, and pepper; cook until potatoes are soft. Reduce heat to low. Add the chopped corned beef, mustard, and butter. Cook, using a spatula to press mixture into bottom of skillet, until browned on one side. Turn mixture, in sections if necessary, and continue to cook until browned on other side. Serve with cooked eggs, if desired, and Boston Brown Bread.

NUTRITION INFORMATION: per serving without egg—protein: 23 g; fat: 22 g; carbohydrate: 22 g; fiber: 2 g; sodium: 910 mg; cholesterol: 75 mg; calories: 378.

Boston Brown Bread

MAKES 2 LOAVES (6 SLICES EACH)

1 cup unsifted all-purpose flour
1 teaspoon baking powder
1 teaspoon baking soda
1 teaspoon salt
1¹/2 cups unsifted whole-wheat flour
1/2 cup cornmeal
2 cups buttermilk
3/4 cup dark molasses
1 cup raisins
Butter (optional)

Wash and dry two empty metal coffee cans. Grease insides of cans well. In a large bowl, sift together all-purpose flour, baking powder, baking soda, and salt. Stir in the whole-wheat flour and the cornmeal.

In a large bowl with electric mixer on medium speed, beat together buttermilk and molasses. Reduce speed to low and gradually add flour mixture, beating well after each addition. Stir in the raisins. Spoon batter evenly into prepared cans. Cover each can loosely with a piece of buttered waxed paper, then top with a large pieces of aluminum foil. Tightly secure the aluminum foil with kitchen twine or a rubber band.

Set a wire rack in a large stockpot and place cans on rack. Add enough boiling water to reach halfway up the cans. Set pot over high heat and return water to a boil. Reduce heat to low; cover and simmer 1¹/2 hours, adding more boiling water if needed to maintain water level.

To serve, remove foil and waxed paper form cans. Turn loaves out onto a cutting board; slice and serve with butter, if desired. To store, let cool completely and refrigerate bread in cans, covered with foil and waxed paper, for up to 1 week.

NUTRITION INFORMATION: per slice—protein: 5 g; fat: 1 g; carbohydrate: 46 g; fiber: 4 g; sodium: 338 mg; cholesterol: 2 mg; calories: 207.

Clam-and-Corn Chowder

MAKES 6 SERVINGS

4 slices bacon, coarsely chopped

1 medium onion, chopped

1 pound russet potatoes, peeled and cubed

1/2 teaspoon salt

1/4 teaspoon ground black pepper

3 cans (6 1/2 ounces each) chopped clams, drained with
   juice reserved

2 cups milk

1/4 cup all-purpose flour

1 1/2 cups fresh or frozen corn kernels

1 cup half-and-half

1 tablespoon chopped fresh parsley leaves

In a 5-quart Dutch oven or heavy kettle, cook bacon over medium heat until crisp and browned. Using a slotted spoon, transfer bacon to a paper towel; drain. Pour fat into a small heatproof bowl. Return 1 tablespoon fat to Dutch oven; discard or freeze remaining fat. Add onion to fat; cook, stirring occasionally, until softened, 2 to 3 minutes.

Add 2 cups water to Dutch oven, stirring to loosen browned bits on bottom. Add potatoes, salt, pepper, and reserved clam juice; stir and cover. Bring to a boil over high heat; reduce heat to low and cook until potatoes are fork-tender, about 10 minutes.

In a small bowl, combine milk and flour. Add to Dutch oven and stir. Return to a boil, stirring constantly, until chowder has thickened. Add corn and half-and-half and cook 5 minutes. Add reserved clams and cook just until clams are heated through. Stir in parsley and reserved bacon. Divide among 6 soup bowls and serve.

NUTRITION INFORMATION: per serving—protein: 22 g; fat: 11 g; carbohydrate: 43 g; fiber: 4 g; sodium: 461 mg; cholesterol: 62 mg; calories: 354.

Chicken Potpie

MAKES 6 SERVING

FILLING

1 tablespoon vegetable oil

3/4 pound boneless, skinless chicken thighs, cut into 1 1/2-inch pieces

3/4 pound boneless, skinless chicken breasts, cut into 1 1/2-inch pieces

1 cup frozen pearl onions, thawed

1 cup thinly sliced carrots

1/3 cup thinly sliced celery

1 1/2 cups frozen peas

1 can (14 1/2 ounces) reduced-sodium chicken broth

3/4 cup milk

1/3 cup unsifted all-purpose flour

3/4 teaspoon salt

1/2 teaspoon poultry seasoning

1/4 teaspoon ground black pepper

1/2 package (15 ounces) refrigerated piecrust or Flaky Piecrust (recipe follows)

FLAKY PIECRUST

1 1/2 cups unsifted all-purpose flour

1/2 teaspoon salt

1/2 cup vegetable shortening

4 to 5 tablespoons cold water

1. *Prepare Piecrust, if making from scratch:* In a medium bowl, combine the flour and salt. Using a pastry blender or 2 knives, cut the shortening into the dry ingredients until mixture resembles very coarse crumbs. Add cold water, 1 tablespoon at a time, mixing lightly with fork, until pastry is moist enough to hold together in a flattened ball. Wrap ball in waxed paper and refrigerate until chilled, about 30 minutes.

2. *Prepare Filling:* In a large saucepan, heat the oil over medium heat. Add the chicken thighs and cook 2 minutes. Add the chicken breasts and pearl onions; sauté until chicken has cooked through and onions are lightly browned, 5 to 7 minutes. Using a slotted spoon, transfer the chicken and onions to a plate and set the mixture aside.

3. Add the carrots and the celery to saucepan; sauté vegetables until slightly softened, about 5 minutes. Stir in the peas and chicken broth. Bring mixture to a boil; reduce heat to low, cover, and simmer 5 minutes.

Heat the oven to 425°F. In a 2-cup liquid measuring cup, stir together milk, flour, salt, poultry seasoning, and pepper. Slowly whisk milk mixture into saucepan. Stir until thickened. (If mixture starts to seize, add a small amount of water.) Stir in the reserved chicken and onions. Spoon chicken and vegetable mixture into 9-inch round baking dish or cast-iron skillet.

Between 2 sheets of floured waxed paper, roll out the chilled pastry to an 11-inch round. Remove top sheet of waxed paper and invert crust over filling. Remove remaining sheet of waxed paper and trim excess pastry crust to fit baking dish. Cut slits to allow steam to escape. Bake until crust is golden and filling is bubbly, 20 to 25 minutes. Let cool slightly and serve in dish.

NUTRITION INFORMATION: per serving—protein: 31 g; fat: 17 g; carbohydrate: 32 g; fiber: 4 g; sodium: 769 mg; cholesterol: 87 mg; calories: 402.

Cozy Oatmeal
MAKES 2 SERVINGS

1/4 teaspoon ground cinnamon
1/4 teaspoon salt
1 cup quick-cooking oats
2/3 cup shredded apple
1/3 cup raisins
2 tablespoons pure maple syrup
2 tablespoons chopped walnuts
Butter (optional)

1. In a 2-quart saucepan, combine 2 cups water, cinnamon, and salt; bring to a boil over medium-high heat. Add oats and cook 3 minutes.

2. Stir in the shredded apple, raisins, 1 tablespoon maple syrup, and 1 tablespoon walnuts. Cook 5 minutes more. Divide oatmeal between 2 serving bowls. Drizzle remaining maple syrup over top and sprinkle with walnuts. Garnish with butter, if desired.

NUTRITION INFORMATION: per serving (without butter)—protein: 9 g; fat: 7 g; carbohydrate: 65 g; fiber: 7 g; sodium: 274 mg; cholesterol: 0 mg; calories: 346.

Fancy Macaroni and Cheese
MAKES 8 SERVINGS

WHITE SAUCE:

4 tablespoons butter
1/4 cup unsifted all-purpose flour
41/2 cups milk
1/8 teaspoon grated nutmeg

MACARONI:

1 tablespoon butter
1/2 cup finely chopped shallots
2 cups sliced white mushrooms
11/2 cups sliced shiitake mushrooms, caps only
3 cloves garlic, finely chopped
1/4 teaspoon ground black pepper
1/4 teaspoon salt
1 pound elbow twists (cavatappi) or elbow macaroni
11/4 cups (4 ounces) shredded Asiago cheese
11/4 cups (4 ounces) shredded Cheddar cheese
11/4 cups (4 ounces) shredded provolone cheese
3/4 cup unseasoned bread crumbs

Prepare White Sauce: In a 2-quart saucepan, melt butter over medium heat. Add flour and stir well. Cook mixture, stirring constantly, 1 minute. Add milk and continue stirring. Increase heat to medium-high and bring mixture to a boil; cook 1 minute more. Remove pan from heat and stir in nutmeg. Cover and keep warm.

Prepare Macaroni: In a 4-quart saucepan, melt butter over medium heat; add shallots and cook 1 minute. Add white and shiitake mushrooms, garlic, pepper, and salt; sauté until all liquid from the mushrooms has evaporated, about 10 minutes. Set mushroom mixture aside.

Cook macaroni according to package directions; drain well and stir into mushroom mixture.

Heat oven to 350°F. In a medium bowl, combine Asiago, Cheddar, and provolone cheeses. Add all but 1/2 cup of the combined cheeses to the warmed sauce; stir until cheeses have melted.

Add sauce to macaroni-mushroom mixture, stirring to combine. Spoon into a 9- by 13-inch baking dish. Sprinkle top with remaining cheeses and bread crumbs. Bake until lightly cooked through, about 30 minutes. Cool slightly; serve.

NUTRITION INFORMATION: per serving—protein: 21 g; fat: 25 g; carbohydrate: 37 g; fiber: 2 g; sodium: 601 mg; cholesterol: 73 mg; calories: 451.

Tuscan Bean Soup with Asiago Toasts

Makes 6 servings

1 tablespoon vegetable oil

1 pound smoked turkey or chicken sausage, cut into
   ^{1}/4-inch-thick slices

1^1/4 cups chopped fennel

1^1/4 cups chopped onion

1 clove garlic, finely chopped

2 cans (14^1/2 ounces each) reduced-sodium chicken broth

1 cans (14^1/2 ounces) can diced tomatoes

^{1}/4 teaspoon ground black pepper

^{1}/2 teaspoon rubbed sage

1 can (19 ounces) cannellini beans, liquid reserved

^{1}/2 cup shredded Asiago cheese

12 baguette slices (^{1}/2 inch thick), cut diagonally

In a 6-quart saucepan, heat the oil and sauté the sausage over medium heat. Cook sausage until heated through, 5 to 7 minutes. Remove sausage and drain drippings, reserving 1 tablespoon drippings in pan. Add the fennel and onion to pan; sauté until softened, about 10 minutes. Add garlic and cook 1 minute. Stir in chicken broth, tomatoes, pepper, and sage. Cook 10 minutes. Add cannellini beans with reserved liquid and reserved sausage. Bring mixture to a boil over medium-high heat and cook 1 minute. Reduce heat to low and simmer 10 minutes more.

Prepare Asiago Toasts: Heat broiler. Mound 2 teaspoons Asiago cheese on each bread slice and place on baking sheet. Broil until cheese and bread are lightly toasted, 1 to 2 minutes. Divide soup among 6 soup bowls; serve with toasts.

NUTRITION INFORMATION: per serving—protein: 33 g; fat: 16 g; carbohydrate: 65 g; fiber: 10 g; sodium: 1,361 mg; cholesterol: 68 mg; calories: 532.

One-Pot Recipes to Warm the Soul

Braised Lamb Shanks

MAKES 4 SERVINGS

2 cups dried Great Northern beans

1/4 cup unsifted all-purpose flour

1 teaspoon paprika

1/2 teaspoon salt

1/4 teaspoon ground black pepper

1/4 cup vegetable oil

4 lamb shanks, about 11/4 pounds each

2 cups chopped onion

5 cloves garlic, chopped

3 cups beef broth

3 cups reduced-sodium chicken broth

11/2 cups dry red wine

1 tablespoon tomato paste

2 bay leaves

1 tablespoon fresh chopped rosemary

1 teaspoon fresh chopped sage leaves

1 cup carrots, cut into 1/2-inch chunks

2 tablespoons chopped parsley leaves

2 tablespoons grated lemon rind

Place beans in a 4-quart saucepan and cover with cold water. Set over high heat and bring to a boil. Remove pan from heat, cover, and allow to stand at room temperature for 1 hour. Drain and set beans aside.

In a shallow bowl, combine the flour, paprika, salt, and pepper. Dredge the lamb shanks in the flour mixture, shaking off excess.

In an 8-quart Dutch oven, heat 2 tablespoons oil over medium heat. Brown lamb thoroughly on all sides. Remove from pan, cover, and set aside.

Pour off fat from saucepan and heat remaining 2 tablespoons vegetable oil. Add onion and sauté until softened and lightly browned, 5 to 7 minutes. Add 3 cloves garlic, beef broth, chicken broth, 1 cup red wine, tomato paste, bay leaves, rosemary, and sage. Bring mixture to a boil over high heat. Reduce heat to low and simmer 5 minutes. Add reserved beans and lamb. Cover and cook for 11/2 hours.

Stir in the remaining 1/2 cup wine and the carrots. Cook until carrots are tender—about 30 minutes. In a small bowl

393

combine the remaining 2 cloves chopped garlic, parsley, and lemon rind.

To serve, divide beans among 4 serving plates. Top with lamb; garnish with parsley-lemon mixture.

NUTRITION INFORMATION: per serving—protein: 109 g; fat: 40 g; carbohydrate: 87 g; fiber: 6 g; sodium: 1,665 mg; cholesterol: 255 mg; calories: 1,214.

Coq Au Vin Blanc
MAKES 6 SERVINGS

MARINADE:

3 cups dry white wine

1 cup chopped onion

1/2 cup sliced carrot

1/2 cup sliced celery

3 cloves garlic, chopped

2 tablespoons olive oil

1 to 2 tablespoons fresh whole parsley leaves

8 whole black peppercorns

1/2 teaspoon salt

6 pounds assorted chicken pieces (thighs, breasts, drumsticks)

COQ AU VAIN:

4 slices bacon, chopped

1 tablespoon olive oil

12 fresh or frozen small white onions, peeled

2 cups carrots, peeled and cut into 1-inch chunks

1 cup sliced celery

3 cloves garlic, chopped

1 shallot, chopped

1/4 cup unsifted all-purpose flour

3 cups chicken broth

1 tablespoon balsamic vinegar

1 bay leaf

1 teaspoon dried thyme leaves

1 teaspoon salt

1/4 teaspoon ground black pepper

1 pound small red potatoes

Prepare Marinade: Combine white wine, onion, carrot, celery, garlic, oil, parsley, peppercorns, and salt in a 3-quart saucepan. Bring to a boil over medium-high heat. Reduce to low and simmer for 5 minutes. Remove pan from heat and let marinade cool to room temperature.

Arrange chicken pieces in large nonreactive container and pour cooled marinade over them. Cover and refrigerate at least 4 hours or overnight.

Prepare Coq au Vin: Remove chicken from marinade and pat dry. Strain marinade and reserve liquid; discard the vegetables.

In a 6-quart heavy kettle or Dutch oven, cook bacon over medium heat until crisp. Using a slotted spoon, transfer bacon to paper towels. Brown chicken parts in bacon drippings in Dutch oven. Remove chicken from Dutch oven and discard all but 1 tablespoon fat. Add olive oil and onions; sauté onions until lightly browned, 8 to 10 minutes. Add carrots, celery, garlic, and shallot; sauté 5 minutes longer.

In a medium bowl, combine the reserved marinade liquid and the flour. Add mixture to the Dutch oven with the chicken broth, vinegar, bay leaf, thyme, salt, and pepper. Return chicken to Dutch oven and cook, covered, for 45 minutes. Add potatoes and cook until potatoes are fork-tender, about 20 minutes more. Divide the mixture evenly among six serving bowls. Garnish each serving with reserved chopped bacon.

NUTRITION INFORMATION: per serving—protein: 61 g; fat: 24 g; carbohydrate: 41 g; fiber: 5 g; sodium: 1,096 mg; cholesterol: 176 mg; calories: 708.

Seafood Gumbo
MAKES EIGHTEEN 1½-CUP SERVINGS—

1 cup unsifted all-purpose flour

1 cup vegetable oil

3 cups diced celery

3 cups diced onion

3 cups diced green bell pepper

7 cups reduced-sodium canned chicken stock

3 cups okra, sliced horizontally into ½-inch slices

1 pound smoked ham, diced

½ pound crab meat

2 cans (28 ounces each) crushed tomatoes, juice reserved

½ cup fresh chopped parsley leaves

1 tablespoon fresh lemon juice

1 tablespoon sugar

1 teaspoon dried oregano leaves

½ teaspoon dried thyme leaves

½ teaspoon Old Bay seasoning

½ teaspoon salt

¼ teaspoon ground black pepper

¼ teaspoon ground red pepper

*2 pounds medium fresh or frozen shrimp, peeled
    and deveined*

½ teaspoon gumbo filé powder

9 cups cooked rice

Hot-pepper sauce, to taste

In a 12-quart heavy kettle or Dutch oven, heat flour and oil over medium-low heat. Cook, stirring frequently, until flour browns to a dark, mahogany color, being careful not to burn, 40 to 50 minutes. Stir in the celery, onion, and bell pepper. Cook, stirring occasionally, until vegetables are soft, about 30 minutes.

Add the chicken stock, okra, ham, and crab meat; cook 40 minutes more. Stir in the tomatoes and juice, parsley, lemon juice, sugar, oregano, thyme, Old Bay seasoning, salt, black pepper, and red pepper. Cook 30 minutes. Stir in the shrimp and filé powder; cook until shrimp have cooked through, about 15 minutes. Serve warm over rice with hot-pepper sauce or freeze for up to 2 months.

NUTRITION INFORMATION: per serving (with ½ cup rice)—protein: 39 g; fat: 20 g; carbohydrate: 42 g; fiber: 3 g; sodium: 788 mg; cholesterol: 156 mg; calories: 512.

Wintertime entertaining can be a cozy affair:

Take the chill off—have plenty of wood on hand to keep a good fire going in the fireplace.

Make sure to have a couple of throws on chairs and sofas to warm up the living room.

Baskets add texture and warmth to a room. They are handy for holding books and magazines as well as an armful of dried bittersweet.

Mix together a group of candlesticks made of different materials such as pewter, brass, and silver plate. When lit, these will add a cluster of light and warmth to any room.

Fruit bowls are flea market classics—set one in the center of your table and fill it with fruit of the moment—a pile of persimmons adds a bold splash of color.

Chili Verde

MAKES 6 SERVINGS

2 tablespoons vegetable oil

1¹/₂ cups chopped onion

3 cloves garlic, chopped

1 jalapeño pepper, seeded and chopped

1 teaspoon cumin

1 pound tomatillos, husks removed and quartered

6 poblano or Italian frying peppers, roasted, peeled,
  seeded, and chopped

3 cups reduced-sodium chicken broth

1 large potato, peeled and cut into 1-inch cubes

¹/₃ cup chopped fresh cilantro

1 teaspoon salt

¹/₄ teaspoon ground black pepper

2 pounds boneless pork chops, cut into 1-inch cubes

In a 6-quart saucepan, heat oil over medium heat. Add onion and sauté until softened, 5 to 7 minutes. Add the garlic, jalapeño, and cumin; sauté 2 minutes longer. Add tomatillos, poblano peppers, and chicken broth. Increase heat to high and bring mixture to a boil. Cook 1 minute. Reduce heat to low and simmer until tomatillos are soft, about 20 minutes. Transfer tomatillos mixture to a bowl and allow to cool for 10 minutes.

Working in batches, pulse mixture in the bowl of a food processor fitted with chopping blade until coarsely processed. Return processed mixture to pan.

Add potato, cilantro, salt, and black pepper to pan. Cook over medium heat until potato is fork-tender, about 15 minutes. Stir in the pork and cook just until pork has cooked through, 10 to 15 minutes. Serve.

NUTRITION INFORMATION: per serving—protein: 52 g; fat: 26 g; carbohydrate: 24 g; fiber: 4 g; sodium: 862 mg; cholesterol: 148 mg; calories: 544.

Country Cooking: Tapping into Maple

Banana-Oatmeal Pancakes with Maple-Rum Syrup

MAKES 3 SERVINGS (9 PANCAKES)

1¹/3 cups buttermilk

¹/2 cup quick-cooking rolled oats

1 cup unsifted all-purpose flour

1 teaspoon baking powder

¹/2 teaspoon salt

1 tablespoon vegetable oil

1 large egg

¹/2 teaspoon vanilla extract

1¹/2 cups coarsely chopped ripe bananas

³/4 cup maple syrup (grade A, if available)

1 teaspoon rum (or ¹/4 teaspoon rum extract)

¹/4 teaspoon ground cinnamon

3 tablespoons chopped pecans, toasted

Heat oven to 200°F. In a small bowl, combine buttermilk and oats. Set aside 10 minutes. In a large bowl, combine the flour, baking powder, and salt.

In a medium bowl, whisk together vegetable oil, egg, and vanilla. Add egg mixture to flour mixture, combining well. Fold in chopped bananas. If mixture seems too thick, add 1 to 2 tablespoons water.

Heat a nonstick griddle or skillet over medium-high heat. Coat with vegetable-oil cooking spray. Spoon ¹/3 cup batter for each pancake onto hot griddle. Cook until tops bubble and edges are crisp, 3 to 5 minutes. Turn pancake over and cook 1 minute more. Repeat with remaining batter and keep pancakes warm in the oven.

In a small saucepan, combine maple syrup, rum, and cinnamon over low heat until warm. Top pancakes with warm syrup and toasted pecans; serve.

NUTRITION INFORMATION: per serving—protein: 15 g; fat: 15 g; carbohydrate: 126 g; fiber: 6 g; sodium: 615 mg; cholesterol: 75 mg; calories: 672.

Cornish Hens with Wild-Rice Stuffing

MAKES 4 SERVINGS

3/4 cup wild-rice blend

2 tablespoons butter

1 tablespoon vegetable oil

1 cup chopped onion

1/2 cup chopped fresh fennel

1/2 cup mixed dried fruit, diced

1/4 cup chopped pecans, toasted

5 tablespoons maple syrup (grade A, if available)

2 tablespoons chopped fresh parsley

2 tablespoons plus 2 teaspoons soy sauce

1 teaspoon grated orange rind

3/4 teaspoon salt

1/2 teaspoon ground cinnamon

1/4 teaspoon ground black pepper

1/4 teaspoon Chinese five-spice powder

4 Cornish hens (about 1 1/4 pounds each)

1 tablespoon orange juice

Cook rice according to package directions and set aside.

In a large skillet, heat 1 tablespoon butter and the oil over medium heat. Add onion and fennel; sauté until softened and lightly browned, 5 to 7 minutes. Stir in died fruit, pecans, 2 tablespoons maple syrup, parsley, 2 teaspoons soy sauce, the orange rind, salt, cinnamon, black pepper, and five-spice powder. Cook until the liquid has been absorbed, 10 to 15 minutes. Remove from heat. Stir in rice and let cool completely.

Heat oven to 375°F. Remove giblets from Cornish hens; wash and pat dry. Stuff hens lightly with wild-rice mixture. Put any remaining mixture in baking dish. Using kitchen twine, crisscross drumsticks and tie together, if desired. Place hens on a wire rack set in a roasting pan.

In a 1-quart saucepan, combine remaining 3 tablespoons maple syrup, 2 tablespoons soy sauce, 1 tablespoon butter, and the orange juice; cook over medium high heat until butter melts and mixture thickens.

Brush mixture onto hens and place in oven. Roast 1 hour. Place remaining wild rice mixture in oven with hens. Cook until a meat thermometer inserted into the thickest part of thigh registers 180°F and rice is heated through, about 30 minutes more. Let cool 10 minutes and serve.

NUTRITION INFORMATION: per serving—protein: 70 g; fat: 24 g; carbohydrate: 41 g; fiber: 4 g; sodium: 698 mg; cholesterol: 234 mg; calories: 667.

Maple-Marinated Roasted Salmon

MAKES 8 SERVINGS

3/4 cup maple syrup (grade A, if available)

2 tablespoons grated and peeled fresh gingerroot

2 tablespoons fresh lemon or lime juice (or white-wine vinegar)

2 tablespoons reduced-sodium soy sauce

1/2 teaspoon ground black pepper

1/4 teaspoon salt

1 salmon fillet, about 2 1/4 pounds (skin on)

Heat oven to 400°F. In a large baking dish, combine maple syrup, ginger, lemon juice, soy sauce, pepper, and salt. Place salmon, skin-side up, in dish. Cover, refrigerate, and marinate 15 minutes. Turn; marinate 15 minutes.

Line a large baking pan with parchment paper. Place salmon on parchment, skin-side down. Brush with marinade and place in oven. Roast salmon 10 minutes. Brush fish with remaining marinade and continue roasting until flesh flakes when tested with a fork, 10 to 15 minutes more. Serve.

NUTRITION INFORMATION: per serving—protein: 34 g; fat: 11 g; carbohydrate: 27 g; fiber: 0 g; sodium: 369 mg; cholesterol: 94 mg; calories: 347.

Glazed Brisket with Root Vegetables

MAKES 8 SERVINGS

BRISKET AND VEGETABLES:

2 tablespoons all-purpose flour

2 teaspoons salt

1/2 teaspoon ground black pepper

1 beef brisket, 4 to 5 pounds

2 tablespoons vegetable oil

1 1/2 cups chopped onions

1 shallot, chopped

2 cans (14 1/2 ounces each) beef both

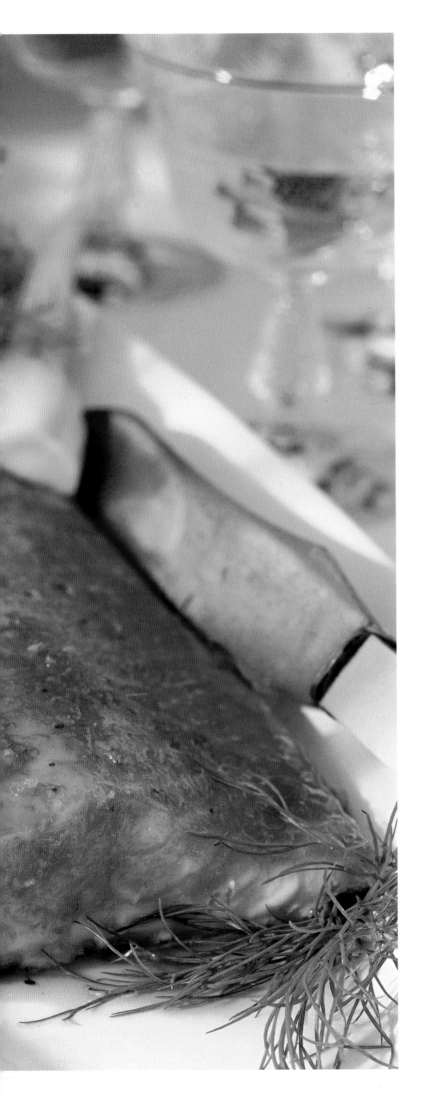

¹/₄ cup balsamic vinegar

¹/₄ cup maple syrup (grade A, if available)

10 whole black peppercorns

5 allspice berries

3 whole cloves

1 pound carrots, peeled and cut into chunks

1 pound potatoes, peeled and cut into chunks

1 pound rutabaga, peeled and cut into large chunks

1 pound turnips, peeled and cut into quarters

GLAZE:

1 can (14¹/₂ ounces) beef broth

¹/₂ cup maple syrup (grade A, if available)

¹/₄ cup balsamic vinegar

1 teaspoon tomato paste

4 allspice berries

2 cloves

Prepare Brisket and Vegetables: On a large plate, combine flour, 1 teaspoon salt, and ground black pepper. Rinse brisket; pat dry with paper towels. Dredge in flour mixture, coating all sides. In an 8-quart Dutch oven, heat oil over medium heat. Place brisket in Dutch oven and brown on all sides. Transfer to a large plate; set aside.

Add onions and shallot to Dutch oven; sauté until softened and lightly browned, 7 to 10 minutes. Stir in beef broth, vinegar, maple syrup, peppercorns, allspice berries, cloves, and remaining 1 teaspoon salt.

Heat oven to 350°F. Bring broth mixture to a boil and remove from heat. Return brisket to Dutch oven, cover, and place in oven; cook 1¹/₂ hours. Add carrots, potatoes, rutabaga, and turnips. Cover and cook until vegetables are fork-tender, about 45 minutes.

Prepare Glaze: In a 1-quart saucepan, combine beef broth, maple syrup, vinegar, tomato paste, allspice berries, and cloves. Bring mixture to a boil over high heat. Cook until mixture thickens and reduces to ¹/₂ cup—about 10 minutes. Discard allspice berries and cloves.

Remove Dutch oven from oven. Place a wire rack in a large baking pan. Place brisket on a wire rack. Arrange vegetables around brisket. Brush brisket and vegetables with glaze.

Increase oven temperature to 375°F. Place baking pan in oven and cook, brushing occasionally with remaining glaze, 15 to 20 minutes, until meat and vegetables are glazed.

Cook remaining liquid in Dutch oven over medium-high heat until thick enough to coat the back of spoon, 10 to 15 minutes. Strain sauce and serve with brisket and vegetables.

NUTRITION INFORMATION: per serving—protein: 75 g; fat: 39 g; carbohydrate: 37 g; fiber: 5 g; sodium: 1,103 mg; cholesterol: 240 mg; calories: 807.

Pear-Maple Upside-Down Cake

Makes 8 servings

1 stick plus 3 tablespoons butter, softened
3/4 cup maple syrup (grade A, if available)
1/4 cup firmly packed light brown sugar
4 pears, peeled, cored, and thinly sliced
2 large egg yolks
1 large egg
1/2 cup sour cream
1 teaspoon vanilla extract
2 cups plus 2 tablespoons unsifted cake flour
1/4 cup granulated sugar
1 teaspoon baking powder
1/4 teaspoon baking soda
1/4 teaspoon salt

Heat oven 350°F. Melt 3 tablespoons butter in a 10-inch cast-iron skillet over medium-high heat. Stir in 1/2 cup maple syrup and the brown sugar. Stir until the sugar dissolves. Bring to a boil and cook for 2 minutes. Remove from heat and arrange pear slices in skillet in a circle, overlapping the slices with wider ends facing out. Set the skillet aside.

In a small bowl, whisk together egg yolks, egg, and 1/4 cup sour cream, the remaining 1/4 cup maple syrup, and the vanilla. Set egg mixture aside.

In a large bowl, combine the flour, granulated sugar, baking powder, baking soda, and salt. With mixer on medium speed, blend in remaining 1/4 cup sour cream. Working in three additions, add egg mixture, scraping down sides of bowl after each. Pour batter over pears in skillet.

Bake until a cake tester inserted in center of the cake comes out clean, 50 to 60 minutes. Let cool 5 minutes and invert onto cake plate; serve.

NUTRITION INFORMATION: per serving—protein: 5 g; fat: 21 g; carbohydrate: 66 g; fiber: 3 g; sodium: 293 mg; cholesterol: 127 mg; calories: 469.

Maple Cream Pie

Makes 8 servings

CRUST:

2 cups unsifted all-purpose flour
1/2 teaspoon salt
1 cup vegetable shortening
3 tablespoons ice water

MAPLE FILLING:

3 large eggs
2 cups pure dark-amber maple syrup
1 cup heavy cream
3 tablespoons all-purpose flour
2 cups sweetened whipped cream

Prepare the Crust: Heat oven to 375°F. In a medium bowl, combine flour and salt. Using a pastry blender or two knives, cut in shortening until mixture resembles coarse crumbs. Sprinkle water, 1 tablespoon at a time, over flour mixture until dough holds together when lightly pressed together.

Roll out dough between two pieces of plastic wrap to an 1/8-inch thickness. Remove top sheet and invert over a 9-inch pie dish. Remove remaining plastic; fit dough into dish. Trim, leaving 1/2-inch overhang. Tuck overhang under, flush with rim of pie dish. Gather scraps of dough and reserve for

Sugar on Snow

It's easy to make maple sugar candies.

Set about a cup of real maple syrup to boil over medium heat, stirring constantly.

While it's boiling, send the kids out for a shallow pan of very clean snow (if no snow use finely crushed ice).

When the maple syrup has reached the soft-ball stage (drop a teaspoonful of the hot syrup into cold water; if it forms a soft ball at the bottom of the glass, it's ready), remove the pan from the heat and pour a thin stream over the snow or ice.

You can even make squiggles or try your hand at letters, flowers, and animals. After the candy cools for about five minutes, it's ready to peel off the snow and eat.

use in Cookie Garnish. Place crust in freezer 5 minutes. Line crust with aluminum foil; fill with dried beans or pie weights. Bake until edges are lightly browned, 12 to 15 minutes. Transfer to a rack; remove foil and weights.

Prepare Maple Filling: In a medium bowl, combine eggs, maple syrup, cream, and flour; whisk until well blended. Place pie dish on a baking sheet; place both on oven rack. Pour filling into crust. Bake until puffed and golden and a cake tester inserted in center comes out clean, 40 to 50 minutes. Let cool.

Prepare Cookie Garnish: Roll out reserved dough between 2 pieces of plastic wrap to an 1/8-inch thickness. Remove top sheet of plastic and invert onto baking sheet; remove remaining piece of plastic wrap. Using a 2-inch maple-leaf cookie cutter, cut out 8 cookies. Bake until lightly browned, 7 to 10 minutes. Let cool completely.

Pipe whipped cream around pie. Arrange cookies on top, stem ends towards center. Serve.

NUTRITION INFORMATION: per serving—protein: 7 g; fat: 47 g; carbohydrate: 80 g; fiber: 1 g; sodium: 191 mg; cholesterol: 149 mg; calories: 764.

Warm Cabbage Slaw with Maple-Bacon Dressing

MAKES 6 SERVINGS

4 slices (4 ounces) bacon, cut in half

1/2 cup apple-cider vinegar

1/3 cup maple syrup (grade A, if available)

1/2 teaspoon ground celery seed

1/4 teaspoon ground black pepper

3/4 cup sliced leeks

3 cups shredded green cabbage

1 1/2 cups shredded red cabbage

1/2 cup grated carrots

In a large skillet over medium heat, cook bacon until crisp. Transfer to paper towels and discard all but 3 tablespoons fat from skillet. Add vinegar, maple syrup, celery seed, and black pepper. Bring to a boil and cook 1 minute. Pour all but 1 tablespoon warm dressing into a small bowl.

Adjust heat to medium low and add leeks to skillet. Cook until slightly softened, about 2 minutes. Add green and red cabbage and carrots. Stir in reserved dressing and cook just until vegetables soften, 3 to 4 minutes. Transfer to serving platter, top with bacon, and serve immediately.

NUTRITION INFORMATION: per serving—protein: 2 g; fat: 9 g; carbohydrate: 18 g; fiber: 2 g; sodium: 155 mg; cholesterol: 46 mg; calories: 158.

Rice Pudding with Macadamia-Maple Brittle

MAKES 8 SERVINGS

6 cups milk

1 cup sugar

2 tablespoons unsalted butter

1 cup medium-grain rice

2 cinnamon sticks (3 inches each)

2 large eggs

2 teaspoons vanilla extract

1/3 cup maple syrup (grade AA, if available)

1/4 cup chopped macadamia nuts, toasted

In a 4-quart saucepan, bring milk, 3/4 cup sugar, and the butter to a boil over medium-high heat, stirring until sugar dissolves. Add rice and cinnamon sticks; return mixture to a boil. Reduce heat to medium low, cover and simmer 25 minutes, stirring occasionally.

In a medium bowl, whisk together eggs and vanilla. Whisk 1 cup of rice mixture into egg mixture. Transfer egg mixture to a saucepan with rice mixture, stirring until well combined. Reduce heat to low and simmer 10 minutes. Remove from heat, discard cinnamon, and transfer to a 2-quart baking dish. Let cool at least 20 minutes or cover and refrigerate overnight.

Heat broiler. In a small bowl, combine maple syrup with remaining 1/4 cup sugar. Press macadamia nuts into rice pudding, covering the top. Drizzle maple syrup mixture evenly over top. Broil, 4 inches from heat, until lightly browned, 2 1/2 to 3 minutes. Let cool, spoon into dessert cups, and serve.

NUTRITION INFORMATION: per serving—protein: 10 g; fat: 13 g; carbohydrate: 61 g; fiber: 0.5 g; sodium: 111 mg; cholesterol: 85 mg; calories: 399.

Fresh Herbs Perform

Waldorf Chicken Salad Sandwiches

MAKES 4 SANDWICHES

1 1/2 pounds boneless, skinless chicken breast

1/2 small onion

5 whole black peppercorns

3/4 teaspoon salt, divided

1/4 cup mayonnaise

2 tablespoons extra-virgin olive oil

2 tablespoons tarragon vinegar

1 tablespoon Dijon-style mustard

2 teaspoons chopped fresh tarragon leaves

1/2 teaspoon ground black pepper

1 large apple, peeled, cored, and cut into 1/2-inch chunks

1/3 cup diced celery

1/3 cup chopped pecans, toasted

2 baguettes (10 inches each)

4 large leaves of red-leaf lettuce

In a 3-quart saucepan, combine chicken, onion, pepper-corns, and 1/2 teaspoon salt with enough cold water to cover. Bring to a simmer over medium heat. Reduce heat to low and simmer until chicken has cooked through, 15 to 18 minutes. Drain and set aside until chicken is cool enough to touch. Discard onion and peppercorns.

In a medium bowl, combine mayonnaise, olive oil, vinegar, mustard, tarragon, pepper, and the remaining 1/4 teaspoon salt.

Chop chicken into 1-inch pieces and toss with tarragon dressing. Toss with apple, celery, and pecans.

Slice baguettes lengthwise and place lettuce on the bottom halves. Top with chicken salad, cover with baguette, and cut each baguette in half to make four sandwiches.

NUTRITION INFORMATION: per sandwich—protein: 44 g; fat: 28 g; carbohydrate: 30 g; fiber: 3 g; sodium: 583 mg; cholesterol: 106 mg; calories: 551.

Sage-Buttered Corn on the Cob

MAKES 4 SERVINGS

4 ears fresh corn, in husks
1/2 stick (1/4 cup) salted butter, softened
1/4 cup chopped fresh sage
1/4 teaspoon fresh-ground black pepper

Prepare the Corn: Preheat grill to medium high. Fill a large bowl with water, add the corn, and soak for 30 minutes. Stir together butter, sage, and pepper in a small bowl and set aside. Cut four 12-inch pieces of kitchen twine and set aside. Drain the corn and, without removing the husks from the ears, pull them away from the cobs and remove the silk to reveal the kernels. Brush each ear with about 1 tablespoon of the sage butter and replace the husks. Tie the husks closed by wrapping the twine around the ear several times and securing it at the top with a knot. Grill, turning corn occasionally while cooking until kernels are just tender—30 to 40 minutes. Untie ears and serve immediately.

NUTRITION INFORMATION: per serving—protein: 6.1 g; fat: 24.9 g; carbohydrate: 39.6 g; fiber: 0 g; sodium: 240 mg; cholesterol: 62 mg; calories: 377.

Herb-Stuffed Grilled Trout

MAKES 4 SERVINGS

4 whole trout (about 1 pound each), gutted and rinsed
    with heads and tails left on
24 sprigs thyme
1 medium-size red onion, sliced into 1/4-inch thick rounds
1 teaspoon salt
1/2 teaspoon fresh-ground pepper
2 tablespoons olive oil

Prepare the Fish: Preheat the grill to medium high. Place the trout on a clean work surface. Evenly divide the thyme, red onion, salt, and pepper among the 4 trout and place in the cavity of each. Rub the outside of each trout with oil and set aside. Cut twelve 10-inch lengths of kitchen twine; tie 3 around the body of each trout to secure the herb stuffing.

Cook the Trout: Place the trout in a large grill basket and cook directly on the grill rack for about 7 minutes. Flip the grill basket over and continue cooking until opaque in the center, about 7 more minutes. Remove the twine and serve immediately.

NUTRITION INFORMATION: per serving—protein: 18.3 g; fat: 21.2 g; carbohydrate: 4 g; fiber: 0.8 g; sodium: 674 mg; cholesterol: 0 mg; calories: 447.

Orange-Spice Granola

MAKES 4 CUPS

1 container (8 ounces) rolled oats
1 1/3 cups sliced almonds
4 ounces whole raw cashews
1/2 cup dark brown sugar
1 teaspoon finely grated orange zest
1 teaspoon cinnamon
1/4 teaspoon ground nutmeg
1 stick plus 2 tablespoons unsalted butter
1/3 cup plus 1 tablespoon maple syrup

Make the Granola: Preheat oven to 350°F. Line a baking pan with parchment paper and set aside. Combine oats, almonds, cashews, sugar, orange zest, cinnamon, and nutmeg in a large bowl and mix well. Melt the butter over low heat in a small saucepan and stir in the maple syrup. Pour the butter mixture over the granola and toss to coat evenly. Spread the granola in an even layer on the prepared baking pan and bake until the cashews are golden and the oats are crisp, 15 to 20 minutes. Cool and store in an airtight container for 1 week or refrigerate up to 1 month.

NUTRITION INFORMATION: per 1/2-cup serving—protein: 3.6 g; fat: 7.6 g; carbohydrate: 15.6 g; fiber: 1.9 g; sodium: 3 mg; cholesterol: 8.6 mg; calories: 140.

How to Best Store Fresh Herbs

Basil, cilantro, and parsley store best in a glass of water for a day or two in the refrigerator.

Pack other fresh herbs in a sealable plastic bag placed in the vegetable crisper of the refrigerator for 3 days to 2 weeks.

Sage and White Cheddar Scones

MAKES 8

4 cups unsifted all-purpose flour

4 teaspoons baking powder

1 teaspoon salt

3/4 teaspoon dried rubbed sage

1/2 teaspoon sweet paprika

2/3 cup vegetable shortening

1 1/2 cups shredded white Cheddar cheese

1 tablespoon grated Parmesan cheese

1 1/3 cups milk

1 tablespoon Dijon-style mustard

1 tablespoon half-and-half

Heat oven to 425°F. Grease a large baking sheet and set aside. In a large bowl, combine flour, baking powder, salt, sage, and paprika. Using a pastry blender or 2 knives, cut in the shortening until mixture resembles coarse crumbs. Stir in 1 1/4 cups Cheddar cheese and Parmesan cheese.

In a 2-cup liquid measure, stir together milk and mustard. Add to the cheese mixture; mix lightly with a fork until the mixture clings together and forms a soft dough.

Turn out dough onto lightly floured surface and knead gently 5 or 6 times. Divide in half. Using lightly floured rolling pin, roll one dough half into a 7-inch round; cut into 4 wedges. Repeat with remaining dough half.

Place wedges, spaced 1 inch apart, on prepared baking sheet. With the tines of a fork, pierce tops. Brush tops with half-and-half and sprinkle with remaining 1/4 cup Cheddar cheese.

Bake scones until golden brown, 15 to 18 minutes. Serve warm.

NUTRITION INFORMATION: per scone—protein: 14 g; fat: 26 g; carbohydrate: 51 g; fiber: 2 g; sodium: 601 mg; cholesterol: 29 mg; calories: 497.

Sweet Potato and Black Pepper Biscuits

MAKES A BAKER'S DOZEN (13)

2 cups unsifted all-purpose flour

2 teaspoons baking powder

1 teaspoon sugar

1/2 teaspoon cracked black pepper

1/2 teaspoon baking soda

1/4 teaspoon salt

3/4 cup (1 1/2 sticks) butter

1 cup puréed sweet potato

2 tablespoons heavy cream

Heat oven to 425°F. In a large bowl, combine flour, baking powder, sugar, pepper, baking soda, and salt. Using a pastry blender or 2 knives, cut butter into flour mixture until mixture resembles coarse crumbs. Stir in puréed potato and cream until the dough is soft.

Turn out dough onto a lightly floured surface; knead gently 5 times. Roll out to a 1/2-inch thickness. Using a 2-inch biscuit cutter, cut dough; place, spaced 1 inch apart, on ungreased baking sheet. Repeat with remaining dough. Bake until lightly browned, 12 to 15 minutes. Serve.

NUTRITION INFORMATION: per biscuit—protein: 3 g; fat: 12 g; carbohydrate: 19 g; fiber: 1 g; sodium: 224 mg; cholesterol: 32 mg; calories: 192.

Savory Quick Breads

The perfect partner for winter meals, these fresh-baked breads bring back the memories of peaceful hours spent in the kitchen. With these quick bread recipes, your kitchen will be filled with those same delicious aromas, without taking all the time for kneading and rising.

Herb Popovers
MAKES 8

6 large eggs
2 cups milk
6 tablespoons butter, melted
2 cups unsifted all-purpose flour
1 teaspoon herbes de Provence
1 teaspoon salt

Heat oven to 375°F. Generously grease 8 seven-ounce oven-proof custard cups; place cups on a baking pan and set aside. As an alternative, use a nonstick popover pan.

In a large bowl with an electric mixer on medium speed, beat eggs until frothy. Beat in milk and butter. Reduce speed to low; beat in flour, herbs, and salt.

Divide batter among prepared custard cups. Bake 1 hour. Using a sharp knife, pierce side of each popover, allowing steam to escape. Continue baking until browned—about 10 minutes longer. Turn out and serve immediately.

NUTRITION INFORMATION: per popover—protein: 10 g; fat: 15 g; carbohydrate: 27 g; fiber: 0.8 g; sodium: 420 mg; cholesterol: 188 mg; calories: 283.

Head into the Woods for a Weekend of Food Adventures

Cranberry Cornmeal Pancakes

MAKES 24 FOUR-INCH PANCAKES

3/4 cup dried cranberries

2¹/4 cups all-purpose flour

3/4 cup powdered buttermilk

3/4 cup cornmeal

3 tablespoons sugar

2 teaspoons baking soda

1 teaspoon baking powder

1/4 teaspoon salt

3 large eggs, well beaten

2 tablespoons vegetable oil

Make the Pancake Mix: Combine the cranberries and 3 tablespoons boiling water in a small bowl and let steep for 15 minutes. Drain the cranberries and set aside. Combine the flour, buttermilk, cornmeal, sugar, baking soda, baking powder, and salt in a large bowl and mix well. Heat a large griddle or skillet over medium heat. Add the eggs, oil, and 2 cups water to the flour mixture and mix well to incorporate all lumps.

Make the Pancakes: Pour 1/4 cupfuls of batter onto the hot griddle to form pancakes. Sprinkle plumped cranberries on the batter and cook until the batter bubbles and the edges of the pancakes begin to crisp. Turn each pancake over and continue to cook until both sides are golden brown. Repeat until all batter is used. Serve pancakes immediately.

TIP: Making the pancake batter outdoors can be time consuming and messy so here is a tip: Premeasure and mix dry ingredients in a large sealable plastic bag to which only a few liquids need to be added. Snip a whole in the corner to create a "piping bag" and squeeze the batter onto the griddle.

NUTRITION INFORMATION: per pancake—protein: 3.6 g; fat: 2.2 g; carbohydrate: 18.4 g; fiber: 0.9 g; sodium: 172 mg; cholesterol: 29.2 mg; calories: 109.

Bacon and Egg Hash
MAKES 4 SERVINGS

1/2 pound slab bacon, cut into 1/2-inch cubes

1 onion, coarsely chopped

1 red bell pepper, coarsely chopped

1/2 recipe Foil-Baked New Potatoes, chopped (see below)

4 large eggs

Make the Hash: Cook the bacon in a large skillet over medium-high heat until browned and crisp. Remove the bacon and set aside. Discard all but 2 tablespoons of the bacon fat; add the onions and peppers to the pan, and sauté for 3 minutes. Add the potatoes and bacon and cook until heated through—about 5 minutes. Lower heat to medium low and gently crack the eggs onto the surface of the hash. Cover the pan and cook until the eggs are set—about 5 minutes. Serve immediately.

NUTRITION INFORMATION: per serving—protein: 20.5 g; fat: 19.2 g; carbohydrate: 25.3 g; fiber: 3.8 g; sodium: 929 mg; cholesterol: 243 mg; calories: 359.

Skillet Biscuits
MAKES 6 BISCUITS

1 cup plus 2 1/2 tablespoons all-purpose flour

1 1/2 teaspoons baking powder

1 1/2 teaspoons orange zest

1/4 teaspoon salt

3 tablespoons vegetable shortening

1/2 cup whole milk

1 tablespoon orange-juice concentrate

Prepare the Batter: Preheat grill to high heat. Heat a large cast-iron skillet with a tight-fitting lid on the grill. In a large bowl, combine the flour, baking powder, zest, and salt. Cut 2 tablespoons shortening into the flour mixture using a pastry blender or two knives until the mixture resembles coarse meal. Using a fork, stir the milk and orange juice into the flour mixture until a loose dough forms. Do not overmix.

Cook the Biscuits: Coat the skillet with the remaining shortening. Drop heaping tablespoons of dough onto the hot skillet. Cover and let the biscuits cook on high for 2 minutes. Reduce the heat to very low or move the skillet to a cooler section of the grill (see Note) and let cook, covered, for 20 minutes. Turn each biscuit over and cook for 10 minutes. Serve immediately.

NOTE: When making biscuits over a campfire, keep in mind that your outdoor stovetop will require a very hot space to initiate the cooking and a warm area to move the skillet to in order to cook the biscuits through.

NUTRITION INFORMATION: per biscuit—protein: 3.2 g; fat: 5.2 g; carbohydrate: 20.6 g; fiber: 0.8 g; sodium: 194 mg; cholesterol: 2.8 mg; calories: 143.

Foil-Baked New Potatoes
MAKES 8 SERVINGS

3 pounds new potatoes, washed and quartered

2 medium onions, cut into 1-inch pieces

1/2 cup parsley, chopped

2 tablespoons olive oil

2 cloves garlic, minced

1 teaspoon salt

1 teaspoon fresh-ground black pepper

Make the Potatoes: Preheat grill to high. Cut two pieces of aluminum foil, each 24 inches long, and set aside. Toss the potatoes, onions, parsley, oil, garlic, salt, and pepper in a large bowl. Place one half of the potatoes in the center of one foil strip and fold the right and left sides of the foil in toward the center to cover the potatoes. Fold the remaining 2 sides to the center to seal. Repeat with the second half of the potatoes and the remaining foil. Place the foil pouches on the grill. Cook until the potatoes are tender—about 20 minutes. Remove the foil pouches from the grill, let sit 5 minutes, unwrap, and serve the potatoes.

NUTRITION INFORMATION: per serving—protein: 4.4 g; fat: 3.6 g; carbohydrate: 24.8 g; fiber: 3.6 g; sodium: 275 mg; cholesterol: 0 mg; calories: 152.

Cold Avocado Soup

MAKES 4 HALF-CUP SERVINGS

1 avocado (about 1/2 pound)

3/4 cup buttermilk

1/2 cup low-sodium chicken broth

1/4 cup plus 2 tablespoons chopped scallions

1/2 clove garlic

1/2 cup water

1 tablespoon lime juice

1/2 teaspoon salt

1/8 teaspoon cayenne pepper

1/4 cup shredded radish

Make the Soup: Combine the avocado, 1/4 cup buttermilk, chicken broth, 2 tablespoons scallions, and garlic in a blender and process until very smooth. Transfer the soup to a large bowl, and while stirring, add the rest of the buttermilk, water, lime juice, salt, and cayenne. Divide among 4 bowls and serve immediately or chill for up to eight hours. Garnish with 1 tablespoon each of radish and scallions.

NUTRITION INFORMATION: per serving—protein: 3.2 g; fat: 8.4 g; carbohydrate: 7.5 g; fiber: 2.5 g; sodium: 337 mg; cholesterol: 2.2 mg; calories: 109.

Roasted Butternut Squash and Pear Soup

MAKES 9 CUPS

1 large or 2 small butternut squash, 3–4 pounds total
1 tablespoon vegetable oil
2 cups chopped onion
1 chopped shallot
1 tablespoon chopped fresh ginger
1 fresh jalapeño, seeded and chopped
1 1/4 teaspoons salt
1/4 teaspoon black pepper
2 ripe pears, peeled, cored, and cut into chunks
6 cups reduced-sodium chicken broth
1 teaspoon honey
1 teaspoon fresh thyme
1/4 cup heavy cream

Roast Squash: Preheat oven 400°F. Cut squash in half lengthwise and place cut side down on a nonstick baking pan. Pour 1/4 cup water into pan and roast for 45 minutes or until squash is tender when pricked with a fork. Remove from oven and allow to cool. (This step may be done the day before preparing the soup.)

Prepare Soup: Remove seeds and peel from roasted squash. Place cooked squash in a medium bowl and mash coarsely. Set aside. In a 6-quart saucepan, heat oil and add onion, shallot, ginger, jalapeño, salt, and pepper. Cook over medium-high heat until onion is soft and begins to turn light brown, about 10 minutes. Add pears and cook another 5 minutes. Measure 3 cups of cooked, mashed squash and add to the saucepan. Stir in broth, honey, and thyme and bring to a boil. Reduce heat and simmer, covered, for 15 minutes. Purée in batches in a blender or food processor, then return the soup to the saucepan. Stir in the cream and keep warm. Do not boil. Serve warm. If you are taking this on a picnic use a thermos to keep it warm. Any leftover soup can be frozen for up to 1 month.

NUTRITION INFORMATION: per serving—protein: 4.3 g; fat: 6 g; carbohydrate: 30 g; fiber: 6.7 g; sodium: 381 mg; cholesterol: 12 mg; calories: 169.

Fig and Brie Turnovers

MAKES 10 TURNOVERS

1 tablespoon butter

2 cups chopped onions

3/4 cup apple cider

1 tablespoon honey

3/4 cup dried figs, coarsely chopped

8 ounces Brie or blue cheese, cut into pieces

Butter-flavored vegetable-oil cooking spray

1/4 teaspoon black pepper

8 sheets of phyllo dough

Caramelize Onions: Melt butter in a large, nonstick skillet over medium heat. Add the onions and cook, stirring occasionally, over medium heat until they are golden brown and caramelized, about 20 to 30 minutes. Set aside.

Hydrate Figs: Combine cider and honey in small saucepan and bring to a boil. Remove pan from heat, add figs, and cover. Allow figs to hydrate until softened—about 1/2 hour. Drain and set aside.

Prepare Turnovers: Preheat oven to 350°F. Dampen a large dish towel. Remove one sheet of dough, lay it on the work surface, and spray with cooking spray. Keep unused phyllo dough covered with damp towel while you work. Cover sprayed phyllo with a sheet of plastic wrap and press to allow the spray to penetrate the phyllo dough. Remove plastic wrap and lay another layer of phyllo over the sprayed piece. Repeat procedure using remaining 6 sheets of phyllo dough. Sprinkle dough evenly with black pepper. Cut the dough (preferably with a pizza wheel) into 5 equal strips. Place 1 1/2 tablespoons of cheese at the bottom of each strip, top with 1 generous tablespoon of chopped figs, and 2 tablespoons of caramelized onion; fold up each one into a triangle shape (as you would fold a flag). Repeat procedure with remaining phyllo strips. Transfer to a nonstick baking sheet and bake in the top third of the oven for 20 minutes or until top is lightly browned. Cool on a rack. Store in an airtight container until ready to serve.

NUTRITION INFORMATION: per serving—protein: 6.9 g; fat: 8.8 g; carbohydrate: 26 g; fiber: 2.4 g; sodium: 393 mg; cholesterol: 20 mg; calories: 207.

Tips for Picnicking and Camping in the Woods

Find a good campsite or picnic spot while there is still plenty of daylight.

Make sure the spot is level with a durable natural ground covering such as dried pine needles and leaves.

To ensure an early start to the day and to save on packing space, measure dry ingredients for batters into plastic bags before leaving home.

Disturb as little as possible. When setting up for a picnic or overnight campsite, opt for a place with a picnic table and an established cooking fireplace or fire ring instead of an untouched area.

Pack a few lightweight, collapsible campstools and cheerful cushions. "Roughing it" doesn't mean you can't include a few luxuries from home.

Camping foods must travel well without refrigeration. A good portable picnic may include hard-boiled eggs, cured meats like salami and pepperoni, hard cheeses, fresh fruits, granola and crunchy flatbreads.

Sit a bucketful of beverages at the water's edge to keep everything cool.

There is a range of camping cooking equipment to choose from on the market. Traditionalists swear by cast iron skillets for durability and even heat distribution.

New, lighter weight cooking alternatives include aluminum, coated steel, and titanium wares made especially for camping.

A footed cooking grate allows air to circulate around the coals making for a more successful fire.

Never do any of your washing directly in a stream or any other body of water.

Strain solids into a large garbage bag and scatter the dirty wash and rinse water widely among brush or stones located 100 feet from ponds, lakes, and streams.

Bugs will be kept at bay the entire time with a good bug repellent.

Clean yourself and your dishes with soaps that are kind to the terrain.

When settling in for the evening, be sure to store all food and toiletries in airtight containers and shake out backpacks and hang them outside of your tent. Woodland creatures have a way of prowling around after dark.

Never bring open food or water into the tent or sleep in clothes you wore while cooking. Some parks may provide you with bear-proof canisters for your campsite.

Many national wilderness organizations strongly suggest using portable camp stoves rather than campfires. In certain parks, cooking fires are only permitted if they are located in an established fire ring.

Always check with the local park ranger about any restrictions before cooking and never leave a fire unattended.

When you break camp, embers must be thoroughly cold. Douse with water, stir the ashes with a stick, and douse again.

425

Wild-Mushroom Tart

MAKES 1 NINE-INCH TART (SERVES 6)

CRUST:

1 1/2 cups all-purpose flour

1/2 teaspoon salt

1/2 cup butter, cut into small pieces

2–3 tablespoons ice water

TART FILLING:

1 cup apple cider

3/4 cup dried porcini mushrooms

3 tablespoons olive oil

1/3 cup chopped shallot

8 ounces white mushrooms, sliced

4 ounces wild mushrooms (such as Cremini, shiitake, or
  chanterelle), sliced

1/4 cup Calvados, applejack, or hard cider

1/2 cup chopped flat-leaf parsley

1/2 teaspoon salt

1/4 teaspoon black pepper

4 large eggs

3/4 cup heavy cream

1 cup shredded smoked mozzarella or smoked Gouda

1/2 cup grated Parmesan cheese

Make the Dough: Combine flour, salt, and butter in a food
processor fitted with metal blade. Pulse until mixture is
mealy, about 6 pulses. Add water, one tablespoon at a time
with processor running, until dough comes together, no
longer than 15 seconds. Gather dough into a rough ball and
flatten into a 7-inch disk and wrap in plastic. Refrigerate for
1 hour minimum or up to 24 hours. Preheat oven to 375°F.

Form the Dough: Roll out dough between 2 sheets of plastic
wrap, creating a circle 2 inches larger than bottom of tart
pan. Remove the top sheet of plastic wrap and turn over
onto a 9-inch tart pan with a removable bottom. Carefully
remove the bottom sheet of plastic wrap. Tuck the dough
into the pan and trim the edges evenly with the top of the
pan. Freeze for 10 minutes. Line the bottom of prepared pan
with waxed paper and weight down with pie weights or dried
beans. Bake 20 minutes and cool on a wire rack.

Prepare Tart Filling: Reheat oven to 375°F. In a small saucepan or microwavable container, bring cider to a boil. Pour hot cider over dried porcini and let hydrate for 20 minutes. Set aside. Heat oil in a large skillet and sauté all fresh mushrooms and shallots about 10 minutes. Add porcini, along with their liquid, and Calvados. Cook on medium-low heat for about 15 minutes or until almost all liquid is absorbed. Stir in parsley, salt, and pepper.

In a large bowl, combine eggs, heavy cream, and cheeses. Stir in mushroom mixture. Pour into the prepared crust. Bake until toothpick inserted in the center comes out clean and top has browned, 30 to 35 minutes. Cool on a wire rack and serve at room temperature. May be prepared the day before and refrigerated. Reheat in a 350°F oven 20 to 25 minutes to bring to room temperature before serving.

NUTRITION INFORMATION: per serving—protein: 25 g; fat: 45 g; carbohydrate: 48 g; fiber: 6.6 g; sodium: 654 mg; cholesterol: 245 mg; calories: 710.

Turkey Club Wrap with Avocado Cream
MAKES 2 SERVINGS

1 whole-wheat tortilla, 12 inches
2 tablespoons Avocado Cream (recipe follows)
1/4 pound sliced roast turkey
5 slices crisp cooked bacon
5 thin slices tomato
3 leaves of red leaf lettuce

Place tortilla on a work surface and spread with Avocado Cream. Layer turkey, bacon, tomato, and lettuce over the tortilla, leaving a border of at least 1 inch all around the edge. Roll tightly, wrap in plastic wrap or foil, and chill until ready to serve. Cut diagonally in half and serve.

NUTRITION INFORMATION: per serving—protein: 25g; fat: 13 g; carbohydrate: 19 g; fiber: 1.6 g; sodium: 453 mg; cholesterol: 63 mg; calories: 295.

Avocado Cream

MAKES 1 CUP

1 ripe avocado, peeled and pitted

2–3 tablespoons sour cream

1¹/2 tablespoons chopped fresh cilantro

1 tablespoon fresh lime juice

1/4 teaspoon salt

1/8 teaspoon ground cumin

1 garlic clove, quartered

Add all ingredients to a food processor and pulse to make a rough purée. Refrigerate until ready to use. Store in an airtight container for up to 3 days.

NUTRITION INFORMATION: per tablespoon—protein: 3g; fat: 2.4 g; carbohydrate: 1 g; fiber: 0.4 g; sodium: 453 mg; cholesterol: 1 mg; calories: 25.

Antipasto Boule

MAKES 6 SERVINGS

VINAIGRETTE:

1/2 cup extra-virgin olive oil

1/3 cup red-wine vinegar

2 cloves garlic, minced

1/2 teaspoon ground black pepper

1/4 teaspoon dried oregano

1/4 teaspoon salt

1/4 teaspoon crushed red-pepper flakes

2/3 cup diced fresh fennel

SANDWICH FILLING:

1/2 cup sliced pitted olives (black or green or a combination of both)

1 can (13.75-ounces) artichoke hearts, drained and quartered

2/3 cup sliced roasted red bell peppers

1/4 cup sliced pepperoncini peppers

6¹/2 ounces sliced salami, julienned

4 ounces provolone cheese, julienned

4 ounces mozzarella cheese, cut into small cubes

1 cup arugula

BREAD:

1 boule-type loaf (crusty round peasant bread), about 12 inches in diameter

Prepare Vinaigrette: In a medium bowl, whisk together olive oil, vinegar, garlic, black pepper, oregano, salt, red-pepper flakes, and fennel. Cover and set aside.

Prepare Filling: In a large bowl, combine all filling ingredients. Add vinaigrette and toss.

Slice the top of the bread. Hollow out the bread and spoon in the filling mixture. Place the top of the bread back onto the boule. Wrap tightly in plastic wrap and let marinate in the refrigerator for 2 to 3 hours or overnight. Cut into wedges and serve.

NUTRITION INFORMATION: per serving—protein: 26 g; fat: 40 g; carbohydrate: 50 g; fiber: 6.8 g; sodium: 1,657 mg; cholesterol: 52.8 mg; calories: 650.

Hit the Trail Mix

MAKES 5 CUPS

1 cup cashews

1 cup dried apricots, quartered

3/4 cup walnut halves

1/2 cup shelled sunflower seeds

1/2 cup golden raisins

1/3 cup dried cranberries

1/2 cup sugar

1 teaspoon 5-spice powder

1/4 teaspoon ground cinnamon

1/2 teaspoon salt

1 large egg white

1 teaspoon water

Prepare the Mix: Heat oven to 225°F. In a large bowl, stir together cashews, apricots, walnut halves, sunflower seeds, raisins, cranberries, sugar, 5-spice powder, cinnamon, and salt. Beat the egg white and water until frothy and fold gently into fruit-nut mixture.

Spread mixture out on a nonstick baking sheet and bake for one hour. Cool on a rack and break apart into pieces. Store trail mix in an airtight container until ready to serve.

NUTRITION INFORMATION: per serving—protein: 7 g; fat: 15 g; carbohydrate: 35 g; fiber: 2.7 g; sodium: 117 mg; cholesterol: 0 mg; calories: 286.

Impromptu Picnics

Sometimes the best moments occur when an outing is impromptu.

Throw a loaf of bread, a wedge of cheese, a bar of chocolate, and a bottle of wine in a picnic basket and you've got the makings of a romantic country interlude.

Layer a jar of pickles, roasted sweet red peppers, marinated mushrooms or artichokes, olives, and cubes of sharp provolone or mozzarella in a plastic container with a tight-fitting lid—Instant Antipasto!

Fill a baguette with slices of brie, fresh basil, and sliced tomatoes from the garden. Top it with a drizzle of honey mustard, wrap it in aluminum foil, and bring along a small cutting board and knife. Once you have found your picnic spot, unwrap the sandwich and slice and serve it on the cutting board.

Pita pockets make for great on-the-go picnic fare: Pair leftover chicken with tomato and arugula, or stuff pita with a salad, dressing and cheese. Wrap each pita in aluminum foil, and to avoid crushing them, stand them upright in a plastic container with a tight-fitting lid.

Crackers, crostini, a round of goat cheese, and a jar of sun-dried tomatoes are a scrumptious snack to toss in your backpack.

Keep a supply of baskets in a range of sizes—small ones can be used for stowing stemware and napkins.

Large baskets can hold piles of sandwiches, cookies, and breads.

Pretty tablecloths and bright napkins and dish towels are perfect for lining the baskets, as well as creating a beautiful table.

Flea markets are great for finding other essentials such
as serving platters, linens, and lanterns.

Best Brownies
Makes 16 brownies

3/4 cup butter

1 1/2 cups sugar

3 large eggs

3/4 cup Dutch-processed cocoa

3/4 cup all-purpose flour

1/4 teaspoon salt

1 teaspoon vanilla extract

1 cup chopped walnuts

Vegetable-oil cooking spray

Make the Brownies: Preheat oven to 350°F. Melt butter on low heat in a medium saucepan. Remove from heat. Stir in sugar. Add eggs, one at a time, stirring well after each addition. In a medium bowl, sift cocoa, flour, and salt together. Add to butter mixture and stir in vanilla and walnuts. Lightly coat an 8- by 8-inch baking pan with cooking spray. Pour batter into prepared pan. Bake until toothpick inserted in center comes out clean, 40 to 45 minutes. Do not overbake.

Remove from oven and cool on a rack. Wrap in plastic wrap and freeze until ready to serve or store in an airtight container.

NUTRITION INFORMATION: per serving—protein: 6 g; fat: 18 g; carbohydrate: 27 g; fiber: 2 g; sodium: 48 mg; cholesterol: 63 mg; calories: 280.

Photography Credits

Jim Bastardo: 186, 188-89, 272-75, bottom: 320

Pierre Chanteau: 241

Eric Crichton/Garden Picture Library: 282-283

Paul Draine: 24-25, 44, 242

Dasha Wright Ewing: 21, 106-107, top right: 107

Richard Felber: 258-59

Mark Ferri: 400-05, 408-09, 422-23, 425-29

Jeffrey Frank: 295

Kate Gadby: 352

Marge Garfield: 284-85

Gridley & Graves: 30-31, 40-41, 52-57, top right: 70, 76-78, 182, 194

Steve Gross: 34, 36-37

Steve Gross & Sue Daley: 16-17, 22-23, 36, 50-51, 70, 91, 106, bottom right: 107, 124-25, 140-41, 144-45, 168-71, 174-75, 210-13, 240, 246-48

Joshua Greene: 296-97

John Gruen: 128-29, 134-35, 224-25

Cary Hazlegrove: 308-09

Tim Hursley, care of House Beautiful: 256-57, 261

Lynn Karlin: 260, 262-63

Doug Kennedy: 326-27

Paul Kopelow: 92, top: 290, 292, 312-13

Mark Lohman: 172-73, 185, 216-19

Michael Luppino: 58-65, 88-89, 162-67, right: 339, 346-47

Steven Mays: 256

Andrew McCall: 80-81, 86-87, 180-81, 226-29

Jeff McNamara: 344

James Merrell: 336-37

Keith Scott Morton: 18-20, 26-29, 32-33, 38-39, right: 40, 42-43, 46-49, 73-75, 82-85, 88, 90, 93-95, right: 101, 105, 108-13, 114-16, 118, 126-27, 132-33, 136-39, 142-43, 150, 152-161, left: 170, 178-79, 183-84, 186-87, 311, 318-19, 328, 330-33, 338-39, 340, 348, 353-55, 362-63, 372, 375-76, 378-81

Charles Nesbitt: 300

Helen Norman: 341

Rick Patrick: 314, right: 315

Judd Pilossof: 392-95, 398-99, 415-17

David Prince: 120-23, 130-31, 192-93, 195-97, 202-05, 208-09, 230-31, 264-67, 286-87, 292-93

Steven Randazzo: 66-68, 71-72, left: 114, 117, 119, 344, 438

Alan Richardson: 268-71, 364-371, 384-87, 389-91, 418-19, 421, 431-33-35

Paul Rochelau: 252-55

Jeremy Samuelson: 198-99

William Bennett Seitz: 190-91

Michael Skott: 146-49

William P. Steele: 79, 250-51, bottom right: 294, 301, 437

Ann Stratton: 410-11, 413

Natalie Stultz: 407

Ron Sutherland/Garden Picture Library: right, 282

Jessie Walker: 34-35, 69, 176-77, 220-23, 288-91, top left: 294, 298-99, 308, 310, 312, 314-15, 316-18, 323

Rick Wetherbee: right, 267

Acknowledgments

We would like to thank the following contributors for their permission to use material adapted from articles that have appeared in *Country Living*.

Michael Weishan: 252-63, 282-87

Debra Muller Price: 24-25, 30-31, 41, 50-51, 70, 79, 80-81, 86-87, 91, 105, 106-07, 130-31, 134-35, 140-41, 144-45, 151, 168-69, 172-73, 180-81, 185, 190-91, 241

Marie Proeller: 21, 124-25, 242

Wendy Lavitt: 22-23, 128-29, 202-07

Larry Rubin: 224-25

Wayne Muller: 216-19

Ellen M. Plante; 220-23

Index